SOCRATES AND THE ANIMALS

Socrates
and the Animals

A Translation by Kathleen Speight
from the Italian
Socrate e le Bestie

by

ELENA QUARELLI

London
HODDER AND STOUGHTON

For permission to use the extract from *Heaven* (The collected poems of Rupert Brooke), the publishers are indebted to the author's representatives, to Sidgwick & Jackson Ltd. (London) and to McClelland & Stewart Ltd. (Canada).

Translator's Preface

As a little girl I remember how distressed I was when, on the death of a pet dog, I was told that it would not go to Heaven, as it had no soul. My feeling against such injustice was almost as great as my grief for the loss of my dog. He had been a very good dog; why could he not go to Heaven? This book gives the answer that I, as a child, would have liked to receive.

But there is no false sentiment about animals here. The author states her position clearly:

'It is easy to fall into the danger of too much sentiment in one's attitude towards animals, and to attribute to their actions human thoughts and feelings, which is quite wrong. But it is just as easy to make the opposite mistake, and to forget that there is a sense of brotherhood in the whole of creation, and that in the heart and mind of any being thoughts and feelings exist which are common to us all.'[1]

And again:

'Each creature is a distinct, individual and irreplaceable note in the harmony of the universe. And if we think that, by imagining that an ant could become a man, we are raising the ant from a position of inferiority, we have misunderstood the genuine, meaningful and essential quality of the ant.'[2]

For each being in the universe has a meaning and a purpose.

From this position she never falters. Dottoressa Quarelli is a philosopher, who approaches her subject with praiseworthy objectivity and lack of prejudice and who searches

[1] p. 87.
[2] p. 28.

for truth by means of exhaustive enquiry and careful, cautious criticism. In seeking to establish the immaterial nature of the souls of animals, her investigations range over a wide field: from Plato and Aristotle, the Bible, the Church Fathers to modern zoologists and investigators of animal psychology, such as Maeterlinck, Jean H. Fabre, and Julian Huxley; while contemporary reviews and her own personal experiences bring lively evidence to support her thesis. Some of these are in humorous vein: as the story of the setter, Topper, who had been taught to eat his bone under the kitchen table, and who learnt the general idea of 'table', for at the command given in another room he went under the nearest one, an elegant spindle-legged tea table, much too small to cover him, so that he stuck out both back and front; or the account of the pug-dog, Dennie, who at the word 'cold' uttered by a shivering guest warming his hands by the fire brought the blanket from his basket and courteously offered it to the visitor. And many are the interesting examples of intelligence in animals, including insects. For instance, two beetles, struggling to free their ball of food from a pin stuck upright in the ground, used their bodies as wedges and levers, and succeeded in doing so; and there is an episode of two rats going along a road, each with one end of a piece of straw in its mouth, and it was found that one was blind and was being led by the other!

Another kind of personal experience drawn upon is the author's discussion with representatives of the teaching of the Church. Here she feels that the attitude is a wrong one, largely due to indifference to the whole question. In fact she finds that the tendency of thinkers in general of the Western world, in contrast to that of the East, has been to lay such stress on the vitalising power of the soul in the psycho-physical compound, and on the fact that man's soul is immortal, that it has established the immaterial nature of the human soul only, and neglected the problem of that of other creatures. A secondary aim is therefore to show how the incorporeal nature of the souls of all creatures, more easily accepted by the East, may also be discussed on the basis of an examination of the ideas of Western philosophy.

The writer found that her enquiry could not be confined exclusively to the animal world; for this had to be seen in the framework of the picture of the universe as a whole, and in particular in comparison with the world of human beings. As a result philosophical problems of universal import are considered, as will be seen from a glance at the interesting list of contents; and the final conclusions take one far beyond the fate of animals, to a meditation on the destiny of the universe. The last chapter is deeply religious and shows how sincerely the author believes in the spiritual apprehension of truths which are beyond human understanding. The materialist, the agnostic or the atheist, and the non-Christian will not follow her so far; but all readers will, I think, be impressed by this thought-provoking book, which, while advocating a deeper sense of man's kinship with all living creatures and a stronger realization of his responsibilities towards them, induces great respect for the animal world and a profound reverence for the mind of man.

Dottoressa Elena Quarelli has also published two volumes of poems: *Prime poesie* (1939) and *In cammino* (1949). She lives at Turin; is married and has two children. In 1954, she founded with her husband the Institute '*Europa giovane*', with the aim of promoting cultural relations between the youth of the countries of western Europe.

In view of what has been said above about the attitude of the Church to her problem, it is interesting to note that '*Socrate e le bestie*' (1958), which is here being presented to the English reader under the title of *Socrates and the Animals*, is now published in Italy by one of the chief Catholic publishing houses, i.e. the S.E.I. (Società editrice italiana) of Turin, which is owned and run by the Salesian order.

Kathleen Speight
Manchester.

Author's Introduction

THE aim of this investigation is to prove, as far as possible on philosophical grounds and with the contribution of the evidence of factual observation, that the soul of animals is incorporeal, that it belongs to the realm of the spirit and is, consequently, immortal.

If one searched for this statement in the field of theosophy and of oriental doctrines, little difficulty would be encountered; in fact it would be like trying to break through an already open door. However, I was interested in the field of dialectics and in treating the subject from the standpoint of the Western tradition of classical metaphysics.

I hope I have reached sound conclusions. The undertaking proved to be difficult at first. I had many very long and cordial, but exhausting, discussions with 'official' representatives of Catholic teaching (who, however, on this subject—I beg leave to say—as if through force of inertia, simply follow a long-established tradition which is not confirmed by true scholarship). I felt as if I had to scale the walls of a fort. On which side was I to begin? Through which opening make a breach? Then I began to realize that the very objections I met with helped to throw light on the subject, and one thing was so bound up with another that the complexity of the problems ended in an ever greater agreement between them; an agreement undeniably in accordance with my first intuition.

I realized in fact that it was not possible to face the problem squarely if I confined the enquiry to the question of animals; without a more universal foundation, it was impossible to build anything solid. Therefore I had to consider it in the wider framework of the more passion-provoking problems which we call 'human'.

All that follows is the result of my modest, but persevering, research. I am not a philosopher by profession; please do not ask of me a more complete historical documentation. I would beg my readers—for I sincerely hope my book will be read—to meditate on all this in the light of simple 'universal' common sense, in the eternal light of reason.

Do not take offence at the first statements that may seem daring. Instead try to follow me dispassionately, if also critically, in my efforts in search of truth. Be willing, if necessary, to revise the most obvious and generally held beliefs on the most weighty problems of the world, beliefs which perhaps did not even seem disputable. Then, perhaps, when you come to the final pages, a flash of intuition may give you that sense of a more complete harmony between Heaven and earth, the transient and the eternal, divine power and divine mercy. These are perceptions which, once we have had a glimmer of them, never leave us.

My intention has been only to sow a seed, to offer a glimpse of the way along which better qualified scholars could travel, going more ably and more deeply into the whole problem.

CONTENTS

xiii

CHAPTER ONE

Classical Philosophy and the Problem

1. *A fundamental principle*

IF, as Aristotle affirms, *the principle governing the behaviour of a being is intrinsic to it*, we cannot deny that animal behaviour, according to reason, derives from a principle inherent in the animal's own consciousness. That is to say: the reasoning power which functions in animals is peculiar to them. And this is confirmed by the very limitations within which this power is revealed.

In other words: this reasoning power does not so much operate 'in' animals, as it is characteristic 'of' animals.

This is a basic principle on which we must take a very firm stand if we wish to avoid the errors of those who try to discredit the idea of a rational and conscious principle in animal behaviour. To acknowledge this, they rightly sense, would be disquieting: for it would upset an explanation which has been put forward for centuries and which is still, through apathy, handed on without ever being subjected to a searching investigation.

* * *

We must come back to the problem with fresh minds, almost as if we were examining it for the first time, with the sense of wonderment of one who is only just discovering God's creatures.

Creation—our own existence and our thought included— is a 'fact', faced with which we find ourselves meditating,

17

thus establishing its truth. Among an infinite number of possible beings, philosophy is never able to declare that the created being such as the bird, the planet, or the plant or even man himself, *must* exist; it can only proceed from the fact that they DO exist. Nor, if we accept *a priori* the laws of the universe according to which everything has its place, can philosophy ever declare of what kind beings must be, except in so far as they are created beings, creatures, and therefore they must be different from their Creator, God.

This does not prevent us, once their existence is established, from recognizing their perfect accord with the harmony of the universe; indeed, this discovery and realization hold endless fascination for us. *But we must be very careful not to regard creatures in an improper way, as if determining them according to a human scheme.* And calmness of judgment will, as a first result, prevent us from falling short of philosophical coherence.

*   *   *

To conclude: we must follow another system altogether. As we reject certain ideas now hardened into habits of mind, logic will return to its rightful place. Among the wonders of creation, an attractive field of enquiry is open to us, a field that we must re-examine with the fresh interest proper to a newly-gained freedom of the spirit.

2. *Plato and St. Thomas*

For centuries St. Thomas's negative verdict has prevailed almost inviolable, a verdict pronounced in all probability not as the result of any special study of the problem. And the reason for such complete, almost blind, acceptance of this position of inviolability is to be sought in the fact that philosophy in the Western world, and particularly *official* Church doctrine, has been very little concerned with the question of the hereafter of animals.

But St. Thomas, who knew how to formulate problems, provides us with another connecting link, most valuable for our speculation, and that is where he notes the consequences which would follow if we observe one of Plato's principles.

'Ancient philosophers,' he says, 'made no distinction between senses and intellect and they attributed to both a corporeal origin. Plato on the other hand did distinguish between intellect and senses; and yet he attributed to each of them an incorporeal origin, asserting that both understanding and feeling are proper to the soul, according to its very nature; and *from this it follows that the souls of "brute beasts"'* (somewhat reluctantly I am keeping to scholastic terminology) *'also are subsisting.'*[1]

*   *   *

Without more ado, I would abide by the decision of Plato, for his logical method conforms so admirably to the dictates of reason. But let us continue to follow St. Thomas's argument, both because it is our duty to be impartial and also because by so doing we shall be able to reach a more complete and a more satisfying and precise statement.

St. Thomas continues: 'But Aristotle established that among the functions of the soul only understanding is exercised independently of any bodily organ. On the other hand feeling and the resulting activities of the sensitive soul are seen to be in action with some sort of change in the body; as in laughter the pupil of the eye is changed, or so it seems, in its colour; and similar changes seem to occur

[1] *Summa Theologica*, p.I, *quaestio* 78, *art*. IV.

in other workings of the sensitive soul. And thus it is clear that the sensitive soul does not possess any active process of its own exercised by itself alone; but all its activities are of a composite nature. *From which it follows that since the souls of the brute beasts do not function by themselves alone, they do not subsist.'*

For once St. Thomas is caught contradicting himself, as can be proved by considering the wider implications of his teaching. For if there is one philosopher who has maintained that the human soul, unlike pure spirits, has been created to exist and function embodied in the flesh, that philosopher is surely St. Thomas.

And it is this characteristic which gives the human soul its own special physiognomy: man who, in understanding and thinking, weeps and laughs, fears and rejoices, takes courage and is disheartened, has his own particular charm, which moves the majesty of God to especial benevolence. (Not for nothing does Holy Scripture say that He delights in speaking with the children of men.) Of such a kind is man, and of such is his soul, an intellectual, incorporeal element introduced into the physical world.

From this St. Thomas deduces that the soul, even after death, yearns for final perfection, for consummation in the blessed resurrection.

But between death and resurrection it survives in its entirety; *this is sufficient to make it quite clear that the origin of the life of the senses is also incorporeal.* And this can never be too often repeated. *It is not the sight-sense which 'sees', but the soul which sees through its senses.*

The active subject is always the soul. It is the immaterial soul which sees, hears, weeps and laughs.

So too for thought. Unless we are materialists, none of us will want to affirm that it is the brain that 'thinks'. Taking a simple comparison, we may imagine intelligence as a source of bright light, whose rays are to be shone through a window-pane. If the glass is bright and clear the rays will pass through without difficulty; if the glass is dull, the light too will appear dim. But the bright light itself is quite unchanged, only it cannot be seen properly.

In all this there is nothing new. It is said, quite truly, that the senses are the windows of the soul. But to be able to see out, to communicate with an outside, windows are necessary only for him who is shut up inside; not for him who is free under a free heaven. The Platonic conception of the imprisonment of the soul in the body has a foundation of truth and throws some light on the mystery of *in what way* the soul may survive independently of the body. (However, such idea of imprisonment is not to be pushed to the point of breaking up the psycho-physical union which makes us into human beings.)

It is certainly true, as Aristotle and St. Thomas assert, that the intellect emerges as having no common measure with the world of the senses. But it is not only the intellect, but the soul in its entirety that is immaterial.

Assuming this to be true, and following St. Thomas's line of argument (or the swing of a mysterious pendulum, which, continually touching its farthest limits, will have to stop some time at the point of perfect balance), is it then true that the active processes of the intellect take place without any physical change?

It is a common experience to note how the expression of the face is moulded according to the workings of the mind, and thought leaves upon it an imprint which is easily visible. Unfortunately it is an even more common experience to note how in certain conditions the activity of the intellect comes to be impeded and even stopped altogether. A clear-cut independence of the intellect from the physical world, therefore, does not exist: as, according to St. Thomas, Aristotle declares it does.

But this is not enough. There is another peculiarity of the human intellect, which denotes that it is human and not angelic; and that is, its method of thought by means of images, however subtle and incorporeal these images may become. In his Aristotelian-Thomist spiritualism Carlo Mazzatini is very insistent on this point: words themselves, even the most abstract of them, as soon as one hears them, take shape as a series of images. Perhaps our minds may go further, to the frontiers of the world of angels, and even as far as the mystery of the meeting with the divinity, following St. John of the Cross, through the most sublime mystical experiences and the most profound theological teaching; but our intellect, in its fundamental structure, remains what it basically is: a human intellect, placed between two worlds, in order to assume the nature of the earth in the life of the spirit.

Returning to the point from which we started, we will conclude that the position taken up by St. Thomas contradicts the implications of his own teaching. *Not even human intelligence is separable from the world of the senses; and yet—as Plato maintains—both intellect and senses are to be assigned to an incorporeal origin.* (We shall deal later with the relationships between consciousness and feeling.)

3. The "Phaedo"

A careful examination of the *Phaedo* demonstrates the accuracy of St. Thomas's interpretation of it. The arguments brought forward to prove the immortality of the soul are in truth so universal as to be able to be applied to the soul of animals as well.

'And what do we think it [i.e. death] is, if it is not the separation of the soul from the body? And is not death this:

on the one hand the body, now become something independent by itself, is severed from the soul; and on the other, the soul, which continues to exist by itself, is severed from the body? What must we believe death is, if not this?"[1]

Such is Socrates' definition of death. And in it a significant difference of wording may be noted. The body 'becomes' something (i.e. different from what it was before), while the soul 'continues' to be what it is. A transformation comes about only for the body; the soul, single and indivisible, even after death does not change its own particular nature. St. Thomas interprets correctly that, from Plato's definition, souls in general, in fact all souls, are immaterial and subsisting; on this point there is no room for any mental reservation whatsoever.

The demonstration then proceeds with the discussion of opposites; a demonstration which, Socrates affirms explicitly, is valid not only as regards man, but 'also with reference to animals and plants', and with the subject of reminiscence, and here it becomes one with cosmic vision: 'If we admit that living things are generated from other beings and not from the dead, and since these living things die, what means have we for preventing all things from being absorbed and consumed by death?"[2]

Later Plato brings out more strongly the strictly philosophical concern, the metaphysical insistence at the base of the theory of reminiscence; that is, the illustration, more or less plausible and necessary (in his eyes also), of a far more essential and universal reality: the participation of the soul in eternal ideas. Here reminiscence is taken in its most immediate sense, as a proof of the indefinite continuation of life.

And even taking into account that we as Christians admit

[1] The *Phaedo*, Chapter IX.
[2] The *Phaedo*, Chapter XVII.

the possibility on the part of God to continue creating new souls, the argument, taken in its entirety as a 'vision' of the world, cannot fail to impress us with its solemnity and lucidity. It calls to mind a passage in the Bible: 'God did not create death, nor does He rejoice in the damnation of the living. For He created creatures so that they might live.'[1] We shall return later to the problem of the origin of death, even though not being able to suggest any solution to it. Let it suffice here to reflect with Socrates and Plato that death cannot be the final word which seals the fate of the world.

'And even after death,' says Socrates, 'the body is preserved, for a period, more or less long, in its original form, and it is certain that at the most it is transformed but not destroyed. Will the soul alone then dissolve into nothingness, the soul which is so immeasurably superior?'

If this were so, we ought to declare, using one of Socrates' own expressions, that 'Nature is lame'.

*   *   *

But let us read again the last conclusive demonstration in reply to Cebes' doubt, a proof which leaves us in eager suspense, as it did those who were listening to Socrates in that last dramatic moment so long ago. Not for the death of him, Socrates, should Phaedo cut his beautiful locks; but he, Socrates, and Phaedo would both shave their heads together on the day that 'this argument of ours shall die and we be incapable of bringing it back to life'; as a sign of deep mourning, for a death far more decisive.

However, the evidence brought forward has not succeeded in dispelling the few doubts which still remain. Evidence of a more universal kind is required; evidence going even more closely into the question of the very nature of the soul.

[1] *Book of Wisdom*, I, 13–14.

And Socrates calmly brings his discussion to a close. Questions, subtle and penetrating, continue to follow one another rapidly, entangling the other speakers more and more in their compelling logic. Let us try to synthesize. Nothing can receive into itself the opposite of what is essential to it. Water can be hot or cold; but fire cannot receive the idea of cold, as heat is not simply a quality acquired by chance but an essential part of its nature. And when a thing finds itself confronted by an essential opposite of this kind, one of two things happen: either it 'flees and yields up its place' or 'it perishes entirely'.

What is by nature the very essence of the soul, if it is not the origin of life? 'Therefore with whatever thing the soul clothes herself, to that thing as she enters it she brings in life.'[1]

Soul means life. And at the approach of death, what will she do? Flee from it or perish. But to perish in this case would be to receive into herself that very opposite quality which her essential nature makes it impossible to admit. Therefore she will flee away and 'safe and uncorrupted she will escape from death'.

Cebes at last declares he is quite satisfied. We have reached the pronouncement which has universal value, and which we too consider valid for all kinds of souls, for souls in their quality of souls, in as much as they are the origin of life. As Socrates declares in a later passage, to speak of 'dead soul' has no meaning. (Thus it is also meaningless to speak of 'mortal soul', an absurd expression which we still continue to use to define the souls of 'brute beasts' without realizing that it is a real contradiction in terms.)

*　　　*　　　*

Such then is the most vast and the clearest conception of

[1] The *Phaedo*, Chapter LIV.

the immortality of the soul which has come down to us from antiquity.

The thought of Socrates and Plato soars aloft solemn and supreme in its self-assurance, finding immediate response in what is most genuine and universal in human consciousness.

4. *Aristotle*

Aristotle goes further, in demonstrating the vital harmony which makes of the soul and body a single creature, and in showing how every genus and every species of being persists in its fundamental structure; such being the order and glory of the cosmos.

But this demonstration, which is in part a completion, should not be pushed too far, and certainly not to the point of obscuring and almost reducing to nothing (as has happened with regard to animals) the supreme achievement of Socrates and Plato; and that is, their theory of the superiority of the soul over the body and its independence of substance, which remains even after separation from the body.

Restless and impatient in his enquiry, which is not free from uncertainties, Aristotle went so far in establishing the intimate union of the soul and body that he compromised the unity of the soul itself, or rather, the unity of that vital centre, the consciousness, to which everything else converges. And he split it up, so to speak, and maintained that only the intellect, indeed only the intellectual agent, is incorruptible. As a consequence it may be to some extent justified to wonder whether he upheld the immortality of the soul, or at least of each individual soul.

From this the Averroists derived their concept of the

universal intellect, against which St. Thomas is later so opposed. Their idea is a mistaken one, but less disloyal to Aristotle's thought than is usually supposed. In fact, to admit salvation of the soul for only the intellect is to call in doubt the individuality, unmistakable and complete, of each human being.

5. The transmigration of souls

As Plato clearly proves, the soul, of any kind whatsoever, is, by its very nature, subsisting. A single, immaterial substance, it persists in its state, while only the body alters, decomposing and changing form.

The subsistence of the souls of animals is therefore also implied in Plato's doctrine. But we can also confirm that it is stated explicitly.

When Socrates, abandoning his strictly dialectic method, discusses possible destinies for souls and mentions transmigration, we find ourselves in the field of pure probability, consciously thought of as such. We shall see, however, how an essential structure of thought also emerges from the myth.

The possibility of transmigration of souls (in the sense of a transition of souls, by means of reincarnation, through different kingdoms, from men to animals and vice-versa) cannot be accepted by classical metaphysics. On this point Aristotle's intuition remains fundamental. The persistence of creatures in the essential forms of their individual beings shows a quality inherent in them which evolution cannot obliterate. "Everything moves on" and "Everything is the same" are two faces of reality.

*   *   *

As St. Francis sensed (and also St. Thomas), each creature is a distinct, individual and irreplaceable note in the harmony of the universe. And if we think that, by imagining that an ant could become a man, we are raising the ant from a position of inferiority, we have misunderstood the genuine, meaningful and essential reality of the ant.

This is a distinction in quality therefore, as in Aristotle. Yet also, in a certain sense, this distinction is only one of extent, when seen in the perspective of a fundamental unity of values. And without this second character, all that there is in the way of communication, collaboration and speech between creatures would disappear. If the intelligence of man and beast did not, from a certain point of view, partake of the same origin, there could be no communication of any sort. And some communication there certainly is. The Gospels bear witness to this, with their frequent comparisons with, and continual references to, the worlds of God's smallest creatures.

*   *   *

This then is the valuable discovery, the positive result emerging from Plato's mistake in considering transmigration of souls a probability: *he sees in all souls what they have in common;* and that is, the fact of their being souls before everything, before the necessary and proper distinctions between them came into being.

He also sees a connection with the human world as regards good and evil.

'Those who chose injustice, and tyranny, and robbery probably take up bodies in the form of wolves and hawks and kites . . . And those people who practised virtue (both private and publicly as good citizens, independently of philosophy or reasoning), those will probably return into a gentle and civilized nature similar to what they had before, as for example that of bees and wasps and ants; or they may return even into their former human shape and from them may be born worthy citizens.'[1]

Here we should note: it is not a question of men becoming ants, or of ants with human souls, as in magic spells or in fairy stories. Plato is speaking of true ants, and true bees; for, for him, only 'souls' really exist. They can take bodily form in men or in bees; but they are in essence always, and only, souls.

*   *   *

This certainty of survival after death, and more than this, the knowledge that the afterlife is the opening of a door to great happiness for all souls, is expressed even more clearly in the comparison of the swans, a comparison illuminated by the gentle smile of Socrates. 'It is a mistake,' he says, 'to think that swans before dying sing because of grief.

'Because of the fear that men have of death, they speak falsely of the swans, saying that when they are singing their last song, they are wailing aloud with sorrow at having to die. But men forget that no bird sings when it is hungry or cold or suffers any pain, not even the nightingale or the swallow or the hoopoe, and these are the birds, which, they say, sing long laments for grief. Therefore neither these birds nor the swans sing for grief, it seems to me. On the contrary the swans, I believe, as sacred to Apollo have a prophetic power, and, *having foreknowledge of the good things they will find in the next world*, on the day of their death they sing and rejoice much more than in any of the days gone

[1] The *Phaedo*, Chapter XXXI.

before it. Now I believe that I myself am a fellow servant with these swans and consecrated to the same God . . . and therefore I think that I shall be able to leave this life with not less gladness than they.[1]

Whether swans have prophetic vision or not, and whether they really sing or not, Socrates' comparison remains significant. Through his words, uttered so smilingly, shines the certainty of a destiny beyond this world, of an inheritance for all its souls. I am speaking of true, individual immortality, and not of a generic return to the 'soul of the world', as some have wished to interpret with regard to animals. The *Phaedo* is too explicit to leave room for any legitimate doubts.

6. *The fate of souls*

It is when one comes to the question of the *fate* of souls that distinctions begin to be made. Merit and unworthiness, the kind and the degree of happiness beyond this world, all this must be adapted to the nature and the capability of souls, and on this point enquiry must be carried out much more thoroughly.

Already in the definition that Socrates gives of wisdom we see the human soul severing itself from the rest and towering up above them, where he says:

'But when the soul proceeds all alone to investigate any problem, then she goes away to the realm of the pure, the eternal, the immortal, the unchangeable; and as she is akin to these, so always is she made fruitful by them every time that she may meditate within herself, and can be made so. Then she is at rest from her wanderings and remains, with regard to them, constant and unchanging; for constant and

[1] The *Phaedo*, Chapter XXXV.

unchanging are those very things to which she clings. And this is the state of the human soul which we call wisdom.'[1]

The human soul then has the power to raise itself, consciously, to the realm of eternity. Nevertheless, this escape from the bonds of the world of the senses in order to attain, in all its purity, the world of ideas is the 'condition' by which man reaches the heavenly blessedness to which he is called, and not the 'necessary foundation' for the affirmation of the immortality of souls.

Moreover we must recognize that in Plato, as the distinction between various natures of souls is not quite clear, the problem of various ultimate fates is not considered. Although he distinguishes between the sensible and the intelligible, unlike Aristotle, he does not appear to admit that there is any nature of soul that has solely a life of the senses. According to him, every conscious substance lives within itself and reflects, in greater or less degree, the life of eternal ideas. We shall see later whether there is any reason to come back to this fundamental intuition.

With regard to *the way in which the after-life is imagined*, Plato is supremely conscious of the difference between philosophical conviction and probability; and it is on this point that he is all too often misunderstood. For we do not differentiate in him the philosopher from the creator of myth, and as a result we underestimate the magnitude of his immortal achievement.

Later developments in his work, as the *Phaedrus* myths, were not held by Plato himself to be indisputable as was his essential doctrine. This is seen in Socrates' hesitation in describing the after-life, where he distinguishes clearly between what seems certain according to reason and what various faiths imagine the after-world to be. A further

[1] The *Phaedo*, Chapter XXVII.

confirmation is also found in a precept expounded in the *Timaeus*:

'Therefore those [i.e. speeches] dealing with a thing which is permanent and proved and clear to the mind must themselves be unchangeable and determined, and, as far as possible, confirmed and irrefutable, and they must lack none of these qualities. But those dealing with a thing which represents that ideal, and is an image of it, must have a degree of credibility in proportion to those others . . . so that when dealing with such things it is useful to accept a myth, probable enough to be believed, without trying to go more deeply into it.'[1]

As I do not possess the inspiration of Plato, I shall not attempt, even in the garb of probability, to foreshadow the life beyond the grave for the souls of animals. But, keeping strictly to evidence afforded by logic, I have so far tried, and I shall continue to try, to make known universal laws concerning them; laws which, stated plainly and without any embellishment, are yet resplendent with a truth that brings us comfort.

[1] The *Timaeus*, Chapter V.

CHAPTER TWO

The nature of the soul of animals. Necessity or freedom of action?

1. *Instinct: Its limitation*

As far as possible, let us try to determine the nature of the soul of animals, particularly with regard to the two essential factors of *intelligence* and *will*.

Do animals show that they are intelligent? Do they show that they understand? Do they give evidence of having any initiative and a will of their own? In what way and how far do they obey instinct? And how far is it true therefore to speak of their freedom of action?

The facts that I have been able to collect are based on my own personal experience and on evidence from various sources; that is, from distinguished writers and from information which has appeared in periodicals and newspapers which I consider reliable. For the most part these deal with observations and experiments carried out in recent years. It is only in the last few years that attention has begun to be focussed on the psychical factor in the life of animals, it now being suspected that our information concerning it is totally inadequate, and that the truth of the matter is far more surprising than we have hitherto thought.

Thus we see how research into the inner workings of the universe always brings us fresh surprises; in fact wonders that make our own flights of fancy seem quite paltry.

When we try to investigate the very essence of things,

reality surpasses our imagination. Therefore I hope that no one will want to accuse me of exaggeration if, when speaking of our little creatures, I endeavour to show that they are much more perfect and complete as regards their inner life than is usually supposed.

We generally belittle any kind of show of intelligence on the part of animals, and, over-simplifying and without much care or thought, we define it as 'instinct'—a magic word which we feel ought to be sufficient to relieve us of the responsibility of having to face up to a delicate problem.

What is instinct, really? I think it might be defined, more or less, as: a primitive and universal impulse which gives features and character to each species of living things. But, it should be carefully noted, though typical of a species, instinct does not destroy individuality in the single members of that species.

Patient psychological observations and studies have revealed quite clearly that the instinct of a species allows freedom of development to a great fullness of life in the individual. Nor is there any contradiction between the instinctive inclinations and the specific way in which the individual responds to them. All this gives rise to a varied and fascinating intermingling—in human beings also—which leads to the characterization of the ego.

We each of us develop our personality in a pattern, if we may so call it, of instinctive knowledge and knowledge deliberately sought, of impulses welling up from the mysterious depths of our being and of our own clear decisions. In this harmonious interplay *the life of consciousness* vibrates and asserts itself.

Among human beings instinct can be concerned with something truly noble, as the sentiment of motherhood, and of sociability (both to be found, too, in animals, if after their own manner). But there is something more: moral law is also instinctive and is an essential part of our soul.

Therefore instinct has a much wider and more complete meaning than the one which is generally attributed to it. In substance this word denotes what is innate, from the instinct of self-preservation to the most common passions: joy, sorrow, hope, despair, apprehension, fear, which are also instinctive in the way they express themselves; and moral law and also—why not?—religious feeling. For man instinctively searches for God, because this desire to see God, this yearning for Him springs from the very depths of man's soul.

So let us not give a too restricted meaning to the term. Instinct does not exclude, on the contrary, it must include, reason and freedom of action; it is not decisive in any absolute way; and each individual responds to it in its own personal fashion.

Returning to St. Thomas's harsh verdict, we should note that in his time it was a commonplace to see in instinct nothing more than the arrangement by which providence assures the existence of the species; thus looking upon it as a *mechanical* and uncontrollable impulse, and making individuals into little more than machines. This is also the point of view of Descartes, less understandably than of St. Thomas, for St. Thomas lived in a moment of history, celebrated for its philosophy, but when the observation of nature did not awaken the interest nor the desire for enquiry that it does in our own day.

St. Thomas says, then, 'It is not possible to detect in the soul of the brute beasts any function superior to those of the senses; in fact they do not understand nor do they exercise reasoning power. This is evident from the fact that all the animals of the same species act in a like manner, as if they acted so because urged by nature and not because of any initiative of their own. In fact every swallow makes its nest in the same way; and every spider weaves its web in the same way.'

And later: 'All pleasures of the brute beasts are concerned with the preservation of the body: in fact they take no delight in sounds, in scents, in appearances, except when these have to do with food and with reproduction, for all their pleasures consist only of these things. Every one of their actions therefore is directed to the preservation of the corporeal being, as if this were their ultimate aim.'[1]

What a summary judgment! It is certain that this inadequate basis of observation has played a very great part in determining the later philosophical thesis. For our part, let us try to provide our evidence more carefully.

2. *Instinct of the species and independence of the individual*

Let us admit the evidence for certain fixed laws in the species, according to which we see that swallows always build their nests in the same way (which is the best way and the most suitable), although this too must be admitted with due reservations and although there is always ample scope for adaptations of these laws. It is providential that it is so.

These things can be seen by the eyes of each one of us. But only the vigilant, patient, keen eye of the naturalist, who has tried to discover the secrets of worlds almost unknown, is able to reveal to us more fully the life which throbs, individually, in each one of even the very tiniest of beings.

In those creatures most closely bound to instinct, their intelligence in digging, weaving, and building (operations which are especially marvellous among insects) can be

[1] *Summa contra Gentiles*, Book II, Chapter LXXXII.

compared, not to that of an engineer who has conceived the general plan of a building, but to the ability, not to be despised, of a clever workman, who often has to solve varied and unexpected problems of a technical order, by overcoming difficulties and inventing makeshifts according to the needs of the moment.

Let us see what Verlaine, the naturalist, noted, when observing in the Belgian Congo a solitary wasp building its tiny cell of clay in which to lay its eggs. I quote from the description by Buytendijk in his *Animal Psychology*:

'While it was busy working, we made various changes to the construction of its cell. We removed what it contained, the lid was often fixed down tightly, or it was taken right away, etc. Verlaine found that any damage that was done was generally repaired by the wasp, but that new situations were not faced up to in the same way. Then the disaster became too great; so the wasp began to build a new cell, using in the end the wall of the old one. It is of the greatest interest to point out in this insect not only its very different modes of behaviour, but also its use of memory. One repair was carried out four hours after the damage had been done and during that time the wasp was unable to go back to its cell.'

It should be noted that the purely human characteristics of perplexity, hesitation, construction, taking down and building up again, are often met with in animals too, though they are usually far more confident than we are in the way they behave. This proves that instinct always leaves room for initiative and for individual industry.

And what must we say about the marvellous phenomenon of the sense of direction, which we have been accustomed to consider as quite instinctive, as if it were a sixth sense? It appears that up to now on this point, too, we have very much over-simplified. Buytendijk says:

'A serious test in favour of the sense of direction theory is to be found in Jung's experiences. Near the Lake of Geneva twenty bees were taken from their hive and carried six km. away to the centre of that region, and then allowed to fly away. Of the twenty, seventeen succeeded in finding their hive. But when carried only three km. away, over the waters of the lake, they were all lost.

'The supposed sense of direction therefore only existed when they were over land, which shows that the bees found their direction by means of their memory and by visual perception.'[1]

Also the latest studies on the language of bees, which is conveyed in the form of a dance, have yielded some very surprising results. When a bee discovers an interesting flower, it acquaints its companions. But, as has been proved, a vague exhalation of perfume is not enough to enable the insects to find the direction to the flower. Much more is needed: for instance, information about the angle of light from the poles, information which, to be passed on and understood, involves the use of the intelligence in a way which would be extremely difficult even for many of us; and which proves once more how the so-called 'sense of direction' is not just something gratuitous, but it requires memory, judgment and even an aptitude for mathematics; in short, an active and personal participation of the intelligence.

3. Of progress in animals

It does not require many examples to drive home the philosophical conclusion. One or two significant ones, chosen from a countless number, suffice to show up the inaccuracy of so many superficial judgments made hitherto.

[1] *Psicologia degli animali*, Chapter IV.

Is it true, for instance, as is often said, that animals do not progress? It should first be stated in reply that, as animals are much nearer to their own state of perfection than we are to ours, in general they have no need for improvement. What is the good of introducing innovations if their habits of life are so well adapted to their needs? Nevertheless, as we have seen, the 'fixed laws' of the species are valid only in a general sense; adaptations of them, and ingenuity on the part of individuals to enable them to cope with an ever increasing number of new and unexpected experiences, only pass us by unnoticed because we are not keen observers.

But there is more evidence. The community of termites, made famous by Maeterlinck's book, shows all the characteristics of a progressive civilization of its own particular kind. This example alone is enough to convince us that we must be very cautious in making certain uncompromising statements, even though for centuries they have seemed quite obvious.

Generally speaking, it is true that the swallow always builds its nest in the same way, and the same with the bee and its hive. Animals are strongly conservative. But this must not be said too hastily and without thinking.

Let us read some of Maeterlinck's statements about the termites:

'This, the oldest known civilization, is the strangest, most complex, most intelligent and, in a certain sense, the most logical and best equipped to meet life's difficulties that has appeared upon this globe before our own. Indeed, though fierce, sinister, and often quite repulsive, it is, from many points of view, superior to that of the bees, that of the ants, and even to that of man himself.'[1] (In fact we have not yet succeeded in finding out by means of what chemical and physical processes the termites obtain some of their results.)

[1] *La vie des termites*, Chapter II.

'It is almost as if Nature had meted out to the termite the same treatment she has to man, by being unjust, malicious, ironical, illogical and treacherous. But to both man and termite this forgetful, wanton, or simply indifferent step-mother has bequeathed one single benefit; a benefit which the termite has turned to good account—as good as, and on occasions even better than, man has—at least up to the present time. This single benefit is a small invisible source of power; a power which in the termite we call "instinct", and in man (without knowing why it should be so), we call "intelligence". With the help of this small force, which has not yet a clearly defined name, the termite has found out how to transform itself, and how to forge for itself weapons which it did not possess, and more swiftly and surely than we have shown ourselves able to forge ours. It has learnt to organize itself, to make itself proof against attack, to maintain the temperature and humidity required in its cities, to render its future secure, increase its population to infinity, and how to become, by degrees, the most tenacious, the most firmly rooted, and the most to be feared of all the occupants and conquerors of this globe of ours.'[1]

Shall we take a look at the termites while at work, and surprise them in one of their very varied occupations? As, for instance, when there is a breach to be mended in one of their extremely solid walls?

'The soldiers, who keep on moving their feelers, seem to be placed in position so as to protect the workers and direct their work. They stand as if drawn up in line at the edge of the opening and step aside the moment a worker comes forward, and they seem to show him where he must place his load.[2]

It appears that termites knew of the advantages of central

---

[1] *Op. cit.,* Introduction IV.
[2] *Op. cit.,* Chapter II.

heating long before we did. They have workmen, soldiers and a complete system of internal police; and also very advanced technical methods.

As ants rear beetles, so termites grow special kinds of fungus, which they find most suitable for food. How did they get the idea of cultivating these particular kinds? Here is Maeterlinck's opinion:

'It is quite clear that originally some fungus must have started to grow on the bits of grass and wood left over which had accumulated in their cellars. They then must have realized that these mushrooms supplied a nutriment much richer, more sure of obtainment, and more easily absorbed than soil or bits of wood debris; also it had the advantage of ridding them of encumbering protozoa which were an aggravation to them. Since that time they have cultivated these cryptogams methodically; and their cultivation has reached such a high degree of perfection that today, by means of accurate weeding, they manage to eliminate from their gardens all the various kinds, and only allow the two varieties of Agaric and Xylaria to grow, which are recognized as the two best. In addition to this, near to their cultivated garden, they get ready secondary or "waiting" gardens, with a store of seeds, ear-marked for rapid growth of a relief crop, with the aim of using these as substitutes for any already sown that suddenly show signs of fatigue or sterility, as frequently happens in the strange world of cryptogams.

'Evidently, or at least probably, all this is due to mere chance; as in the same way quite by chance they hit on the idea of growing the fungus in mounds as being the most practical method; and that this is so we know from the mushroom beds cultivated in the outskirts of Paris.

'Moreover let us note that the greater part of our own inventions may be attributed to chance. It is almost always some indication, some suggestion from nature that starts us off. We then have to turn the suggestion to good account right away and develop the consequences of it; and this is what the termites did, so cleverly and so methodically, as we ourselves would have done. When the case in question refers to something man has done, it is called a triumph of intelligence; when it refers only to a termite, it is put down to a power in things or the genius of nature.'[1]

Therefore, *faced with the reality of facts, it is not exactly true to say that animals do not progress.* There is a certain possibility of improvement open to them, though it is much less necessary for them than for man. It seems that we must be extremely cautious with negative assertions.

Meanwhile Maeterlinck does not hide his bitterness. It is all very well to make due distinctions (i.e. between man and the animals); but why two completely separate systems of weights and measures? There is fundamental injustice in our way of judging animals.

4. *Public and private life in animals*

The termites' city may be taken as the perfect realization of the communist state. Material progress has been achieved to a remarkably high degree (it seems—or so Maeterlinck argues—that termites have found out the secret of how to change the physical characteristics in embryos, so as to obtain from them different individuals according to the functions for which they are destined). But in this state the individuals are valued only from the point of view of their productivity in favour of the community. And this community is a machine, of which all its members are cogs; a machine which crushes immediately anyone who may cause the slightest hindrance to its working.

[1] Maeterlinck, *op. cit.*

This goes for the 'queen', watched over by the courtier-warders; and she is subjected to the tremendous strain of having to lay eggs continually; and then she is left to die of hunger at the first sign of weariness or decline. This goes too for the 'guards', who are unable to feed themselves because of their absurdly long beak-like part which prevents them from picking up any kind of food at all with their own mouths. They are fed so long as they are of use, and they too are allowed to starve as soon as their strength begins to fail.

The state has no tender feelings for the individual.

Like a breath of fresh air, more 'human' I would say, are the homes of the bees and the ants, where lively and cheerful activity is maintained by a greater harmony, by a sense of solidarity and of mutual assistance.

And lastly—still keeping within the realm of insects, as they are more easily classified under this aspect—there are those who are democratic, independent, and free citizens; those who have a private life of their own, a house of their own, fruit to their taste and grown by their own labours (which perhaps has to be protected against profiteers); a loyal female friend or fiancée to pay court to, a small private capital consisting of provisions for themselves and for future offspring. And there are, too, social relationships, friendships and even contracts for work . . .

All this little world is seen in movement in a detailed episode from Fabre. It must not be omitted, for it is enough in itself to sum up many varied aspects of these tiny lives of which we are quite unaware.

Many beetles are kept very busy making up their food into precious balls: no easy task. They have to be worked into a dough, made nice and smooth, and formed so that they will roll properly. It is curious but in the world of insects, as well as in ours, there are shirkers and speculators; there is the beetle who is not very fond of work. And after he has endeavoured to get possession of one of these balls ready-made, and failed, he tries to put another scheme into effect. He goes politely up to another beetle, already in possession of his treasure, and offers to help him to transport it. The other one accepts the offer, without renouncing in any way his status of lawful owner. The sense of ownership is also very keen among animals. Therefore the owner keeps for himself the predominant position of the one who pushes the ball along from the ground. The other beetle from the top of the ball will lighten his labours (more or less effectively, but some show of helping has to be made). Fabre noted this same difference of position many times and made certain that it was always the rightful owner who pushed the ball from below.

As long as the road is on the flat they carry on with common consent; but when the ground begins to rise, the shirker follows an infallible plan of action. He pretends he has fallen asleep (shamming is a weapon often used among animals) and, flattening himself against the ball, he lets himself be rolled along with it. His friend does not protest: he does not trust his assistant very far! He had in reality accepted his help simply because he did not want to say 'no', and thus hoping to avoid worse troubles. This does not prevent the fact of being two together from perhaps turning out to be very useful in a predicament: when, for example, exerting themselves together as much as they can, they may overcome enormous difficulties, as for instance, go up a steep incline, which would be quite impossible with the efforts of one alone.

The end of this partnership, or, better, the unfolding of the drama is most interesting and amusing. As they arrive at the place that the 'owner' considers satisfactory, he stops and begins to dig himself a nice quiet dining-room.

But the 'assistant' makes no further offer of collaboration

in this no less important enterprise. He stays there crouched against 'his' (or almost now 'his') ball, waiting for the digging—as it proceeds—to take up more and more of his friend's attention in the subsoil. When he decides the right moment has come, he sets the precious booty in motion and off he goes as fast as his legs can carry him.

The victim peers out of the hole for a moment. One can imagine his feelings! But not losing heart, he gives chase at once. He may even succeed in catching up with the bandit at some yards distance; but the other shows his great presence of mind. ('Learn wisdom from the children of darkness': is it irreverent to apply the Gospel warning to beetles?) With the most natural and innocent air imaginable, the thief quickly takes up his position as assistant again, pretending that he had only been holding the ball safe after it had slid away. The ground was so flat . . . could it possibly be otherwise? However, unfortunately, wisdom is not always a characteristic of the honest. The 'lawful owner', after some hesitation, swallows the story and accepts the apology as sincere. They both take back the load to the first place, until the irremediable happens: the assistant takes more careful precautions and this time succeeds in getting away with the ball scot-free. The victim of the theft is completely bewildered, as is to be supposed, even if the most inner feelings of beetles are not easily revealed to the human eye; but then, with the resignation of a strong character, he starts his long labour all over again; and this time, let us hope, without any assistant.

Here serious problems of an ethical order occur. Why is the poor beetle allowed to be so unjustly robbed? The need for a higher justice must also be felt among animals. But justice is not of this world: is justice a passport to another world for all creatures?

This is a question which we shall take up later.

5. *Reaction to the unexpected*

Leaving aside these assertions for a moment, let us turn our attention to an experiment carried out by our naturalist, during similar events. For it answers those doubting us, who say that animals behave simply and naturally in all their affairs, merely by following their instinct. But what happens when they are confronted with the unexpected?

At a certain point in the journey of two beetles, Fabre intervened so as to baffle them. Let us tell the story in his words.

'Many times I have subjected two beetle partners to the following test so as to judge their inventive powers when up against a serious obstacle. Let us suppose they are on a level piece of ground, the attendant motionless on the ball while the other is doing the pushing. Taking care not to disturb the outfit, I take a long sturdy pin and pin down the ball to the ground, and it stops rolling immediately. The beetle, quite ignorant of my villainy, doubtless thinks it is a natural obstacle of some sort, a rut in the ground, a blade of grass, or a little pebble blocking the path. He redoubles his efforts, struggles as hard as he can: the ball does not budge. What is happening? Let's go and see. Two or three times the insect goes all round his ball, and not finding anything to explain why it will not move, he comes back again, and gives another shove. The ball is quite immovable. The beetle climbs on top of it. But up there he only finds his immobile colleague, for I had taken care to push the pin in deeply enough to hide its head in the ball's bulk. He carefully examines the top and gets down again. Vigorous shoves are given at the front, and on the sides; again without success. Certainly no beetle ever found itself confronted with such a problem of inertia.

'Then the beetle climbs up and shakes his colleague curled up on top, and says to him something of this sort: "What are you doing up there, you slacker? Get down and have a look, the thing's not working!" But he does not succeed in stirring him; for, for some time yet, I see the one beetle trying to move the immovable, and then examining the machine that has stuck, while the assistant goes on taking it easy. However, at last it begins to dawn on him, too, that something unusual is happening. He realizes it by his companion's agitated pottering about and by the motionless state of the ball. He climbs down therefore and has his turn at examining the problem. But the team of two gives no better results than the efforts of one alone. The matter is becoming complicated. The small fan of their feelers expands, closes, opens again, trembles and shows all the signs of their lively concern. Then a stroke of genius brings this dilemma to an end. "Who knows what there is underneath it?" The ball is then carefully examined at its base, and a little digging soon brings the pin to light. They immediately recognize that here is the crux of the problem.

'Then the two colleagues, one on each side of the ball, push themselves underneath it, and as these living wedges thrust themselves in, it begins to slide up the pin. The softness of the material of the ball, which gives, forming a groove below the head of the immovable pin, admits of this clever manoeuvre. Very soon the ball is suspended at a height equal to the thickness of the beetles' bodies. The rest is more difficult. The beetles at first squat down, then gradually stretch themselves up on their legs, and keep on pushing with their backs. It is hard to manoeuvre, for the higher they stretch up the less strength they have in their legs; but at last they do it. Then comes the moment when a shove with their backs is no longer possible, as they have reached the highest limit they can stretch. There is still one more method, but not so easy for the deployment of their strength. Having taken up their team positions, that is, one with its head facing upwards, the other downwards, both insects push hard, one with the front legs and the other with the back legs. At last the ball falls on the ground, if the pin is not too long. The slight disembowelling of the ball by the pin is then more or less repaired and the transportation begins once more.

'But if the pin is too long, the ball, still firmly fixed, ends by hanging at a height that the insects cannot reach, even by stretching. In this case, after vainly going round and round the inaccessible tree of plenty the beetles leave the field defeated, unless we have the kindness of heart to bring the matter to a close by giving them their treasure back again. An accurate use of wedge and lever: such is the important mechanical feat that the beetle is capable of in order to set rolling again his ball that had got stuck.'[1]

6. *Doubt in animals*

Hesitation, doubt, remorse, buried deep down within our consciousness, are typically human emotions. But interesting observations can also be made regarding them in animals, as we have already seen with reference to hesitation (I would remind you of the various attempts of the wasp who was trying to build its cell).

One evening, when in the country, we suddenly discovered a kitten under a small armchair in the sitting-room. He was not known to anyone, and had never been seen before. Where had he come from? He was a thin, very small kitten, but quite sure of himself as he showed immediately

[1] J. Fabre, *Le monde merveilleux des insecte: 'Le scarabée sacré.'*

by the complete self-possession with which, as an unexpected guest, he took command of the situation.

In one thing, however, he had hardly any self-confidence at all: in jumping from the armchair to the sofa. And yet the seats were low and near together, and for a cat such a jump ridiculously easy. But he couldn't trust himself. He would have liked to jump it; made a gesture as if about to; then drew back and pondered deeply, taking stock of the distance and measuring it against his strength. To those who do not believe that animals have the faculty of judging, I must state that here I actually saw a cat 'judge distance' with all the seriousness of a land surveyor. And for a considerable time. He made as if to take the plunge, then thought better of it; started calculating again, measuring the distance, judging his own strength . . . until, as always happens when one thinks about a thing too much, he did not jump at all.

I could not enter into his little head. But what is certain is that here was a real kind of deliberation, of inner struggle. 'Shall I jump or not?' was the problem that engrossed that kitten. How far did it act by implicit ideas and judgments? I cannot say. But it is certain that that little cat, *in its own way*, pondered, hesitated, reflected and finally came to a decision.

* * *

We are not yet on the level of Hamlet. We cannot quote examples of animals overwhelmed by mental anguish. But who knows what they are 'thinking about' during the long hours when they are quite still. After all we really know nothing at all about it.

There have been cases of suicide among animals; which means that, with greater or lesser awareness of what they were doing, they have in some way or another asked themselves whether it was worth while to go on living.

D

7. *Unicellular creatures and initiative*

It would be easier to continue by demonstrating individual characteristics accentuated in the 'superior' animals. However, I was anxious to begin with those held in very low esteem, as for example, insects, which we most often consider as entirely passive and guided solely by instinct. But we may go further; for traces of intelligent personal initiative have been found even in unicellular creatures. I must confess that at this I was amazed and incredulous at first, but now I am convinced that it must be so, if "nature is not lame". If a beginning of consciousness in souls is acknowledged, Nature could not, in her profound coherence, disappoint us even with regard to these lowest of creatures.

Chapter II of Buytendjik's book, quoted earlier, is entitled: 'Psychology of unicellular organisms'; and here I report one of the most noteworthy of Jennings's experiences:

'A large amoeba C had swallowed a smaller amoeba B; but a tiny channel had been left open and along it the small amoeba was making unsuccessful attempts to flee, following the movements of the large one. At last the small one succeeded in getting quite free; and at this the large one changed its course, seized B and surrounded it completely. The small amoeba then contracted into a little ball and stayed quite still up to the moment when, because of the movements of the large one, it was covered by only a very thin layer of cellular substance. This thin layer was quickly passed through, and the small amoeba then broke away and afterwards was not chased by the large one again.'

And again:

'Now, as has been described by Jennings, the amoebae pursue their prey, and when they fail to catch it by using one method, it appears that they try another one.

'These numerous test reactions, from which emerges an action leading to a definite aim, are found frequently both in unicellular creatures and in superior organisms.'

Thus experiments carried out on a stentor (a genus of infusoria) produced this conclusion:

'The change of behaviour in the stentor, in relation to its earlier manner of acting, is a phenomenon that can be compared in some ways to a kind of apprenticeship in a superior type of organism. From what we can confirm by evidence, it appears that the behaviour of the stentor shows, in an elementary fashion, phenomena which in superior organisms are discernible in an extraordinary, surprising and complicated way. One single difference there is, however, and that is that in the stentor the experience only lasts for a very short period.'

Does a psychical life exist, then, even in unicellular creatures? The judgment of psychology confirms the philosophical deduction.

'The behaviour of unicellular creatures under the influence of both natural and experimental conditions is well worth our attention and particularly because this concerns the question of whether these unicellular creatures differ in principle from the pluricellular. If this were so, as far as concerns superior organisms which possess a nervous system, we could accept a psychological development of their method of behaviour and, refuting any idea of a psychical life for unicellular ones, try to trace *their* functioning back to purely material processes. But there exists no difference in principle between unicellular organisms and the lower pluricellular ones; and therefore reason compels us to admit that all living organisms start off from an identical base in the development of the same processes.'[1]

[1] Buytendijk, *op. cit.*, Chapter II.

It will be objected that in this connection only need for food and the instinct of self-preservation come into play. And it is certain that the more one goes down in the scale of living things, the more is their horizon limited to the elementary laws of existence. But never is it so limited as to shut out altogether a glimmer of something which we may call the life of consciousness, or the life of the spirit, although it is present here only in its most primitive and primordial flickerings.

CHAPTER THREE

Feeling, Consciousness, Knowledge

1. *The conscious self*

HAVING acknowledged that animals have freedom of action, let us try to individualize the make-up of the conscious self, which is the root from which their will and their actions stem.

In order to define this root of being, we will say that the soul, whether angelic, human or animal, is first and foremost consciousness. This is the keystone on which depends the judgment of any kind of psychical manifestation whatsoever.

Consciousness, however confusedly or dimly felt, however rudimentary it may be, is the indestructible principle of unity and consistency which makes, of every creature that is endowed with it, a whole world to itself.

Consciousness causes every sensation, beginning with physical ones, to be perceived. And in this very common fact of perceiving even in a most simple external contact (take, for example, the wing of a flying beetle lightly brushing past a blade of grass) there is something which makes an impression, which goes down, deep as an abyss.

For feeling, however external and physiological it may be, is registered by a *quid*, which is necessarily outside matter, by a point that is not in space (though being in relationship with space), by that immaterial substratum which alone is capable of this perceiving.

Let us take for example an animal which is hungry. Hunger is a sensation transmitted to the brain by the nerves, and then appraised by the conscious self. If the nerves are in a state of atrophy or the brain in a stupor, consciousness cannot appraise the sensation. It is like a wireless receiving station to which nothing has been transmitted. But when the sensation *is* transmitted, the perception of it is made solely by the consciousness. (However, the efficiency of the transmission by the nerves does not always meet with a correspondingly lively disposition in the consciousness. On the other hand consciousness is only in a position to perceive faintly what the nerves are not sufficiently capable of transmitting fully. If the basic relationships are not kept well in mind, these interconnections may lead to the mistake of placing the sensation-conscious self in the physical world.)

We all have the possibility of meditating on this datum from experience. A physical pain, transmitted by our senses, is perceived by the conscious self, by the immaterial ego. If this were not so, why should we be so sorry for those in pain? Why does physical suffering, both our own and that of others, fill us with horror and dread?

Our senses transmit, but it is *we* who suffer. Christianity, with its clearly stated and essential spiritualism, does not make much difference between physical and moral suffering. It recognises that each kind of suffering is an act of the 'soul'. The spiritual ego, qualified in so many ways by matter—but this is a term which must be reconsidered, since a thorough analysis leaves it with very little of its traditional meaning— by its nature dominates matter, transforming it, at the very moment that it becomes conscious of it, into something that transcends it.

Let us admit that the importance of the sensation is proportionate to the value of the ego that perceives it. Differences may result from this. But it does not alter the fact that *the perception of a sensation, for any conscious self whatsoever, is characteristic of an immaterial source.*[1] And this affirmation must, necessarily, be extended from the world of human beings to the animal world also.[2]

The nerves of the dead frog, which gave rise to Galvani's discovery, reacted in an extraordinarily lively way to a slight touch of the rod. But this reaction was not transformed into feeling, precisely because it remained in the domain of the purely physical: there was no consciousness there to impart sensation.

Let it be noted, therefore, how the definition 'sensitive souls', sanctioned by St. Thomas, has, even in its inadequacy, a significance which the angelic doctor himself did not realize. Indeed, to use the very term 'sensitive soul' means to open wide the way into the depths of a conscious self.

2. *Feeling and consciousness*

Let us pass on to a subject no less momentous. The feeling 'perceived' by the conscious self has the character of a kind of inner duality. For while I perceive the feeling, *I know I am doing so*, even though I do not actually realize it by thinking about it.

Are animals perhaps endowed with a kind of feeling which does not experience this objectivity in the consciousness?

Philosophy has made a distinction between perception and

[1] This essentially immaterial character of feeling explains how feeling comes to have so great a part in artistic creation, and also, how clearly, by the process of analogy, a higher spiritual conception may be expressed by an image from the physical world. For in the unity of consciousness the physical and spiritual worlds are in perfect relationship one with the other.

[2] From this it follows that animals too are liable to feel pain; and this fact ought not only to arouse our pity, but also make us realize our sense of responsibility for it. As will be stated later, it is not right to make them suffer.

'apperception'; but it remains to be seen how far such a distinction is legitimate. I believe, in fact, that this '*knowing that I am perceiving*' is radically essential to the fact of perceiving. Here we are entering into the very heart of the mystery of consciousness. For it is quite another thing to turn one's attention to one's feelings and reflect upon them. To do so is typical of human nature, but it is an advance and a going more deeply into things.

The sensitive soul does not simply register passively as would a gramophone record. When actual thought is absent, one can at least still speak of *awareness*, which is a 'knowing', together with the very act of 'perceiving'.

Let us restate what we know concerning our own inner experience, and that of animals as far as it is evident to us. We find:

1. that the perception of a sensation, simply because it is an act of perceiving, is a conscious act (belonging to a consciousness, the possibilities of which extend far beyond what would be involved within the limits of sensation alone, because these possibilities extend towards the justificative sphere of the rational).

On the other hand, in sleep and in certain pathological conditions, we have examples of a dimly-felt consciousness; but if this consciousness disappears altogether, then the sensation also disappears.

2. The behaviour of animals is that of lively and wide-awake creatures; and for this reason we cannot consider attributing to them only a kind of passive perception (even if such a thing were possible, and not, as it actually is, a contradiction in terms).

In a certain latent sense (in so far as it has an implicit quality) their perception is, on the contrary, extremely lively and wide-awake; so much so that it becomes imprinted on their memory.

3. *Consciousness, memory, intelligence*

Not only does their memory preserve and recall perceptions registered in the course of time, but animals also link together various perceptions they have received and behave themselves accordingly, following a connection between cause and effect.

On this way of linking together and bringing into connection various perceptions, a way typical of animals, we base our whole system for training them; as we also base the psychological experiments which have been carried out for some time now, with great seriousness of purpose, so as to ascertain the degree and the characteristics of their intelligence. (An intelligence that philosophers, as is the duty of philosophy, bring into question; but which psychologists, working on data produced by experiment, acknowledge even to the point of feeling the need to study it.)

Having admitted consciousness as both the passive and at the same time the active agent of the perceptions, from it we see the structure of the intelligence taking shape, an intelligence proper to, and characteristic of, animals. In fact, placing this immaterial, incorruptible, conscious soul as common denominator, the question arises: what is the specific difference? And if animals are intelligent, in what way does their intelligence differ from that of man?

CHAPTER FOUR

Language and the Beginnings of Knowledge

1. *Do animals speak to one another?*

INTELLIGENCE is normally revealed through the medium of language and speech is a sign of the intelligent being.

Animals do not speak, or so man has always maintained. But language, as a means of conveying thought, is not necessarily the language of words. The barking of dogs, mewing of cats, neighing of horses and the twittering of birds all present various inflexions of a speech which undoubtedly has meaning in the animal world. Just as the quivering of feelers and the vibration of wing coverings among insects are all signs by means of which they pass on messages and convey definite information. One need only read any article on insect life to form a good idea of this.

When the queen bee dies in a hive, all the hives in the vicinity are immediately informed, and they show this by unusual excitement. When an ant comes across a piece of food too big for it to carry by itself, it goes off and a short while afterwards it comes back with helpers. And often a stray dog, who has found someone kind enough to give it something to eat, will turn up again later, bringing its friends with it.

Therefore language, through signs which can vary a very great deal indeed, is always the expression of thought among animals, as among human beings, and sometimes of a very definite and unmistakable thought. A typical example, already mentioned, is that of the language of bees, which takes the form of a dance.

2. *Do animals gather the meaning of man's language?*

What part has language in animals' relations with man?

In actual fact, the superior animals at least, the animals nearest to man, are able to understand us, up to a certain point, and even to gather the exact meaning of certain words. Indeed it should be noted that animals like us to talk to them. They are sociable creatures and are fond of our company. In this respect, too, there is no real gulf between us; for a bridge may always be thrown across it to make the distance less noticeable.

Man can understand animals (without completely solving the mystery of them); and animals, within limits, understand man, even in certain subtle psychological shades of meaning which one would not expect.

I shall offer only a few examples, for we can all recall many in our own personal experience.

My aunt used to have a lovely greyhound, somewhat quiet and reserved in character, and it was never demonstrative in any way with anyone but its master and mistress. Although it loved going out for walks, there was simply no way of making it go with anybody else, not even with my mother. However, one day my aunt did not feel well, and she said to Mother: 'I really don't feel like going out at all today; do take Elsí for a walk.' And these words sufficed to bring about the desired effect: Elsí immediately followed Mother as obediently and submissively as one could wish.

Another example, not directly confirmed by any member of our family, but given me by an eye-witness and absolutely true, is the following: A huntsman was out with friends and an old dog, which had been his faithful companion for many years. When talking about the dog to his friends he said: "He's getting very old; I shall have to shoot him." At these words the dog disappeared and his master never saw him again.

What meaning do animals give to our words? As we see from these examples and from our own common experiences, they give them *the same meaning that we do*.

Parrots provide an interesting case. It is generally held that they repeat indistinctly and monotonously just what they have heard said. It is true that they repeat sentences exactly as they have heard them spoken, but not just at random. For when they are not saying something over and over again for their own enjoyment, they come out with the sentence most appropriate to the moment and to the occasion. So even if they have not formulated that sentence themselves, the very fact that they use it just when its words acquire a meaning shows that they have a fair knowledge of their general gist. In fact the case of parrots ought to be taken into greater consideration.

3. *Universal concepts*

So as to have a clearer idea of the extent to which animals give meaning to our words, I will now quote a series of incidents, which have appeared in a magazine,[1] and are important as tending to establish in animals the *existence of universal ideas*. This has been much disputed, and it is a problem of great importance; for herein lies the crux of many arguments that I have had to sustain up to the present time. Animals do not stop at the immediate impressions of the *hic et nunc*. It can be confirmed that universal concepts are really present in their minds.

[1] *Reader's Digest*, April, 1950. The reader must not be surprised if I quote examples and facts already widely known. For it is my intention to draw logical deductions from what we can all easily confirm.

I will quote from evidence signed G.E.

'Up to what point are animals able to generalize the meaning of words? For example, to a dog, does the word "table" mean anything more than one single object with which it has some particular thing in common?

'A lady who owned an English setter called Topper used to give him bones to be eaten in the kitchen. When giving them to him, she always said: "Table, Topper," and Topper took his bone to be eaten underneath the kitchen table.

'One day there was a large party in the drawing-room, and on the floor there were various little paper baskets full of sweets. Topper helped himself to some of these. His mistress hurriedly said: "Table, Topper," meaning that her dog should go and chew his sweets under the kitchen table. But Topper went off to an elegant, neat little table near at hand, and, not without some difficulty, he squashed himself beneath it; and, with his head sticking out at one side and his behind at the other, he calmly began to chew his sweets. Quite clearly for Topper "table" was something generic and not only the table in the kitchen.

'I invited the lady and her dog to my study and there I gave him a bone. At her command he immediately took it under the study table. We tested him with all kinds of tables. He always went and put himself beneath the nearest one, never under a chair—though it might be nearer than the table—nor did he ever go into a corner.

'Some weeks later the lady telephoned me to report further. She had been in a field behind her house with her dog and he had dug up a bone. At this without thinking, she shouted, "Table, Topper." Right at the bottom of the field, away out of sight, there was an old table which they had used for picnics. Topper knew this, and so off he went to that old table and there, beneath it, he gnawed his bone.'

Further evidence:

'My grandfather boasted to a guest that our pointer, Strom, would go and fetch his cap for him.

' "And suppose he couldn't find it, what would he do?" asked the visitor.

'Grandfather put his cap in his pocket, and then went out of the house, taking the visitor and the dog with him. After a minute or two he said: "Strom, I want my cap."

'The pointer bounded back into the house. The two men waited. Nearly ten minutes passed before Strom came dashing back. He ran straight up to Grandfather and put into his hand what he had brought out, and stood there barking joyously. He had brought him Granny's straw hat.'

And again:

'Every evening my great-aunt used to put her pug-dog, Dennie, to bed in his basket, and while she tucked him up in his little blanket she always used to say: "There, now, Dennie, won't feel the cold."

'One icy cold evening a cousin came to call. He sat right on top of the fire, rubbing his hands, and talking about the weather. He kept saying that it was cold, cold, simply frightfully cold.

'Dennie slunk out of the room.

'Then we heard the noise of something being dragged downstairs. And here comes back little Dennie, to offer the visitor the blanket from his basket!'

Therefore, for the dogs mentioned above, the words 'table' and 'hat' do not correspond merely to this or that particular object; they mean precisely what we understand by them, that is, they correspond to the 'idea' of those objects, which become individualized each time they are met with. In the same way the meaning of 'cold' for Dennie goes quite beyond the immediate sensation of the present.

Therefore, by a procedure analogous to our own, the intelligence of animals, like our own intelligence, obtains from empirical knowledge a universal idea; an idea which later will guide its intelligence in recognizing the *hic et nunc* when these are presented to it.

I have quoted these particular examples for their obviousness. But examples of the kind are continually before the eyes of us all. One case alone would have been enough to deduce a philosophical axiom; for either the universal concept exists or it does not.

And if we think for a moment, 'to shoot', 'to go out', in fact all verbs, recall universal concepts; so do adverbs, so do adjectives. Without universal concepts speech would have no meaning.

4. *Abstract ideas*

It will, in fact, be pointed out to me that 'table' and 'hat' are ideas of concrete things; so what about abstract ideas?

We will state that the spiritual quality of the universal concept does not vary fundamentally by being referred to something abstract or something concrete. *It is the universal concept which is abstract in itself.* The idea of a 'thing' or of 'justice' can only have place in the mind.

It is sufficient for the tiny ant or the very lowest kind of grub to have the 'idea' of food, to demonstrate the spiritual —and I repeat *spiritual*—nature of its soul. Otherwise the foundations of metaphysics would collapse.

The specific difference between 'abstract' and 'concrete' concepts is to be found in the object to which they refer.

Abstract concepts refer to eternal ideas; and therefore are so irreplaceable and necessary that one cannot conceive of any break in continuity between the various 'worlds'.

5. *Beginnings of knowledge*

The difference here, too, between men and animals is to be found in the fact that, most likely, concepts in animals remain implicit (but this does not make them any the less definite). For animals have no experience of the human activity of formulating, developing and comparing opinions and thoughts.

The treasure of their metaphysical knowledge (for strictly speaking it is metaphysical: because to judge is, according to the law of cause and effect, to perform a metaphysical act) is an untapped source.

Indeed we must enlarge upon Thomist doctrine with regard to this point. It is by experience and observation that we begin to know external objects, or, rather, created things, which might or might not exist. These things we must get to know separately, one by one (although at the same time abstracting from them the 'idea') so as to know that they exist. And this meeting with external objects, which urges us to form judgments based on our first principles, develops, clarifies and *makes us recognize and objectivize* to ourselves the principles of our own judging.

But no one can *discover* what has always existed—except in the sense of tearing away the veil that obscures it from his consciousness—because this is identified with God. The light by which we recognize and judge the world is derived from an inaccessible source.

And *from this very same source, and from no other, can the* vis aestimativa *of animals be derived*. The light which gives light to man illumines the whole of the universe. And its creatures cannot help but be conscious of it and live it, each one in its own particular fashion.

He who acknowledges God cannot conceive of the world in any other way than this.

CHAPTER FIVE

Are Animals Capable of Virtue?

1. *Evidence of behaviour compatible with goodness*

GOODNESS is not possible in any being lacking freedom and knowledge.

Having recognized a freedom of action in animals—even if it is directed along the main road of instinct—and a beginning of knowledge, can we now tackle the question: are animals capable of virtue?

In the *Nichomachean Ethics*,[1] when considering friendship, one of the noblest and most spiritual of sentiments, Aristotle says:

'Friendship is a virtue, or at least it accompanies virtue . . . It is to be found not only among men, but also among birds and among the greater part of living things . . .'

If logic still has value, it follows from this that Aristotle recognizes that animals have a certain capacity for virtue, or at least for 'something that accompanies virtue'.

To a keen observer many instances of friendship among animals may be revealed, instances in which this feeling becomes real self-denial. I once knew two female cats, one of which behaved towards the other just like an elder sister. She humoured the little one in all her whims. She let her take her food from her saucer. She allowed her to go off with her toys (usually very jealously guarded) and then later she would go and get them and put them back in their proper place. And all the time she used to make little moans and mews of protest. This was, then, not just a spontaneous,

---

[1] *Nichomachean Ethics,* Book VIII.

careless impulse of generosity, but a kindness that seemed to involve a real sacrifice; a sacrifice of a kind to satisfy the most severe ascetic. And when the little one died, her friend kept looking for her continually, day after day; she was in fact what could be described as beside herself with grief.

In *L'Idea Zoofila*[1] Guglielmo Bonuzzi relates the following:

'Still within the category of demonstrations of affection ranging from love to friendship, we can here relate, keeping strictly to actual facts, what a student of animal psychology, Professor Nicolò Grillo, observed one day in Genoa. Two large dappled horses stood side by side harnessed to a cart which was standing waiting. Suddenly one of them tried to rub its knee with its lips, evidently because the knee was itching; but it could not reach it because its harness was in the way. Its companion looked at it . . . and then an extraordinary thing happened. The first horse lifted its knee as high as it could, and the other bent down its head, and thus succeeded in licking the itching knee, to the obvious satisfaction of the interested party; for soon afterwards it put its hoof down again.

'What mysterious signs had these two animals used to communicate with each other? And another detail must be added which completes and clarifies the psychological process: the horse that had 'benefited,' shall we say, turned towards its obliging friend, and gently licked its muzzle with its lips; and its companion was not slow to return this crude sort of kiss.'

Still dealing with mammals, the scientist Frederick Clivier tells how a dog died of a broken heart on the death of a lioness, who had been its great friend and companion in a circus; and similarly he heard of the case of a lion who met the same end because of a bitch.

[1] May, 1953.

And now an incident in which an example of moral strength could truly be given the name of virtue:

'My grandfather was out one day driving his pony and trap when all of a sudden the pony stopped, without any apparent reason. He tried to urge it on with gentle persuasion; but the horse would not move. Then he tried shouting at it; again without success. At last he had to have recourse to the whip; but with no better result. So finally he got out of the trap to see what was the matter; and there he found that there was a little child between the pony's hooves.'

And should we not note, too, the sense of responsibility with which animals carry out their work? (As for example the horses drawing sledges, so well described by Jack London.)

And again: one of my acquaintances, when a young man, was out driving in a carriage with his father, when the horse suddenly stopped. Here too, there being no apparent explanation for this behaviour, the driver tried to urge the horse on. But he could not make it budge. So they both got out of the trap to see what was wrong, and they found that there was a thick log of wood right across the road. The horse by itself could easily have got over it; but evidently it was kept back from fear of upsetting the carriage; which was again a fine proof of intelligence and of a sense of responsibility.

If we wish to go into psychological subtleties, here is an example: a little puppy, Leda, did not like her mistress patting another pup, Lola. On the other hand she was quite a polite little soul and did not want to let people see that she disapproved. So every time that Lola tried to get near her mistress, Leda playfully got in the way, just enough to achieve her end, but without losing any of her dainty charm of manner.

Should we not note too the innumerable little trials of patience borne by animals, which go almost unnoticed, and which irritate man so much?

Also, it is not true to say that all cats are treacherous. On the contrary, although I have no reason for saying this, I feel that such an attribute seems only suited to cats of some time ago. Their species appears to have made notable progress along the road to perfection. See with what an air of restraint and forbearance they let people pick them up! They do not always like this, by any means, and on such occasions they make me think of that act of mercy which has been called 'bearing patiently with nuisances'.

Poor pussies, they let people get hold of them without a single protest, and they bear this for a while with great self-control until, as soon as the right moment comes, they decide to escape, and with the utmost relief. And not even the tiniest bit of a claw comes out to scratch. Patience, courteous condescension, complete self-restraint, what more do you want?

Yet the heroes of such feats are capable of deeds of quite a different order.

In the country we once knew a black cat who was always hungry, for he had no home. So absolutely famished was he, in fact, that whatever we gave him (beginning with tasteless soup—tasteless, that is, from the cat's point of view) he finished it all off right away without once lifting his head up from the plate.

One day I took out a paper bag full of good things for another cat, a little cat that had hardly grown at all, for he had such a little appetite. Just as I got out the black cat appeared. 'That's the end of that,' I thought to myself. 'He'll not leave the little one even a crumb.' But the black cat went towards his microscopic rival and then stood still a bit away from him, and he watched him eat as much as he wanted.

And it was only when the little one had had enough that he came forward, and then soon made a clean sweep of everything that was left.

Nor are rats less worthy creatures. And it is with a tale about rats that I must finish if we want to end with a morally enlightening story.

'As he was coming home from work one day a Carnegie miner was surprised to see two large rats on the crown of the road in front of him, each of them holding in its mouth an end of the same bit of straw. A savage impulse took him, and throwing at them a piece of wood that he happened to be carrying, he hit one rat and killed it. When he got up to the two rats he was amazed to see that the other one was still standing there without moving. Then he bent down to examine it, and he found that it was totally blind. Its companion had been leading it with the piece of straw.'[1]

2. Remorse

As regards the other side of the picture one ought also to be able to show that animals are capable of wrong-doing. Here, fortunately, my supply of examples is somewhat meagre; for, as a rule, animals are well-behaved.

Of course fleas bite, and tigers lay traps for their prey. And besides doing these things because of the laws of nature, it might very well be that they take an evil delight in doing them. The lion, a much more trustworthy animal than the tiger, offers an example of a very different kind.

Monkeys play spiteful tricks; but they realize when they have gone too far. My father had one that took to pieces all the electrical appliances in a room (every single thing connected with electricity!); and then, terrified at what it

[1] *L'Idea Zoofila*, May, 1953, art. cit.

had done, it kept in hiding for three whole days. It finally gave itself away by a little bit of tail seen sticking out of the bookcase.

It is well known that elephants and wild beasts in general nurse resentment for many years, until they can avenge themselves. But then they wreak their vengeance with such calm and determination that it is unlikely that they feel any emotional disturbance afterwards. On the other hand, it is very probable that animals are upset after a sudden outburst of uncontrolled anger or of unpremeditated violence.

Domestic animals, we know, go and hide or show that they are frightened after they have done something which transgresses their master's laws. But, even if this is a fine proof of their awareness, it can always be objected that such emotions are caused by practical reasons, from the fear of being punished. What would be more interesting to establish in animals would be a real inner grief, a feeling more 'spiritual' in character; but such signs are far more difficult to discover in these mysterious little minds.

Nevertheless, I once happened to see a dog suddenly give way to his canine instinct with a female cat, who was a great friend of his, and whom he always treated very gently. But this time he chased her off rudely and refused to share a bone with her. Immediately afterwards however, he went and squatted down beside her, with all the air of one who is sorry and in disgrace. He seemed afraid to revert to his usual high-spirited and friendly, easy manner. I *felt sure* that he was sorry for it, that is all that I can say. Certain happenings cannot be proved by documentation; for they are the throbbings of a soul.

Similarly one night I saw a most well-behaved cat, an excellent mother of four kittens, suddenly go for one of the little ones, with frantic screams, as if she were going to kill it. Was she perhaps exhausted by them all?

Soon afterwards she was herself again, and she began to look for the kittens which we had hidden in a cupboard. But she went about it timidly, seeming ashamed of herself, as if she were well aware of her recent fit of madness. As in the case of the dog, her state of mind is not easy to describe in a 'concrete' fashion. I can only report the impression of sorrow and melancholy humiliation that the poor thing gave. She went about, calling her kittens, but a little uncertainly, as if she knew all the time that it was her own behaviour towards them that was to blame. The kittens, meanwhile, were mewing continually inside the cupboard; but when the mother passed close by them, calling them, they stopped immediately.

Next morning we restored three of the kittens to the mother, but we gave away the one she had attacked in the night. She started taking care of the three most diligently; but at the same time she seemed to know that one had disappeared, and she began to call it softly. But it was as if she did not dare to do so loudly and openly. There was an air of utter dejection and humiliation in her behaviour, almost as if she realized that it was just and right that the fourth kitten should be taken from her.

Can animals do wrong? And if so, how far are they aware, objectively, of having done so? I do not wish to go further into this delicate problem. I will content myself by saying that a sensitive soul, such as they evidently possess, is like a feeler, which is quick to receive impressions from every direction.

3. What is virtue?

In order to state more precisely what this 'something similar', something natural to virtue is, which animals show they possess to quite a remarkable degree, we shall have to try *to define virtue*. Such a definition I would formulate as follows: *a willing acquiescence in the ethical laws which govern the world, and a compliance with them which is at least implicitly conscious*. It then remains to clarify 'ethical' laws, the aim of moral philosophy, a definition not at all easy to arrive at.

However, on the ethical plane *recognized as valid for the human spirit*, let us try to find the point of discrimination: that is, *in animals' actions (and habits) which are objectively in accordance with ethical laws, how far do consciousness and freedom have a part?*

Freedom of action and consciousness, or intelligence, are so closely intermingled that it is difficult to conceive of the one without the other; and experience of the one implies experience of the other. All the same I will try to examine them separately, each according to its own particular aspect and manifestations.

According to the Thomist pronouncement, animals are free in so far as the discriminating sense that animates them is intrinsic to them; but they have no free will, as they have no faculty of judgment. Or better, they judge (according to the *vis aestimativa*) by following, *of necessity*, their own sensitive representation of objects.

If such were the case, one could no longer speak of liberty of action; for liberty, an inner, personal, autonomous impulse, derives from judgment. The catch which releases the spring of the will can only be judgment, a decision indicated by intelligence, with which a voluntary act must be connected. Otherwise we have unconsidered acts, not acts freely decided upon.

It is very difficult to support the view taken by St. Thomas. In fact the 'necessity' mentioned above disappears when one admits an intrinsic sense of discrimination and a consequent freedom. If the *vis aestimativa* freely passes on into action, how can we still find place for the 'necessary' link? On the other hand it would be legitimate to speak here about 'spontaneity', a characteristic of the behaviour of animals, which is perhaps responsible for the Thomist ambiguity.

If the angelic doctor, at the price of contradicting himself, admits in animals a certain freedom of action with a sense of discernment, *it is because a being capable of making a decision, even if only implicitly, is inconceivable without freedom of action.* When we say that a creature 'understands', we suggest that it possesses a faculty which is personal, individual, non-transferable and freely exercised, in as much as it is autonomous. With the very fact of 'understanding', a being establishes itself as an individual entity, as a force, however great or small, standing facing the rest of the world, and it derives the reason for its action from its inmost being (in a relative sense, that is). And this reason for action must be derived voluntarily, otherwise it would not be true action.

The fact that certain intuitions, sometimes inexplicable to us, may come up from their inmost being, as if through some mysterious contact with the 'soul' of the world or of the species, or even through the reception of a spiritual telepathy unknown to us, does not in any way deprive the being which is endowed with consciousness of its fundamental liberty and autonomy.

4. *Characteristics of virtue in animals*

We all talk about goodness, truth and beauty, as of things quite familiar. But how many of us would be capable of giving an accurate definition of them? Yet our familiarity with them indicates that the human soul has a sure, instinctive knowledge of universal realities: a knowledge which, however dim or obscure, comes from divine reality itself. It cannot be otherwise.

So, before analysing in our thought and putting into words what virtue is, we already know 'in a certain way' what it is. And we are sure of what we know (the soul is always truthful); we know it deep down in the very origins of our being. Yet it is very difficult to define it. But in our endeavour to define it, in our effort to make it clear to ourselves, we are guided by this dim knowledge that we possess; and this effort of ours tends to 'recognize' something that is concealed within us, *not to 'construct' what no created being could ever give life to*.

Such is the special structure of human knowledge, complex and implicit, which by means of experience and of speech becomes clear to itself; which from the particular leads to the universal, but which could not even give a name to the particular if the universal did not enlighten it.

Ask yourself this question: could it not be that the soul of animals, still such a mystery to us, might have a form of knowledge which approaches ours? With a reasoning power infinitely more limited (which, however, gives rise to the hesitation characteristic of human thought and action) and which, within these limits, might be so much more direct, spontaneous and surer than ours?

The problem of knowledge crops up here again, as we deal with the question of virtue: which latter is, as we have tried to define it: behaviour which is voluntarily and consciously in accordance with divine laws.

Aristotle insists on the need for knowledge and decision to bring about goodness. He says:

'Finally, for virtuous actions it is sufficient to have certain qualities so that they may be performed with justice and temperance; but it is very necessary for the person performing them to behave in a certain way. In the first place, he must know very well what he is about; secondly, he must act with intention, he must act with the avowed intention of doing what he does; and thirdly, as he performs the action, his will must be steadfast and not change.'[1]

This description of *human* virtue seems to have been given on purpose to put obstacles in our way, and to make people say: 'Yes, animals' actions are, *objectively*, consistent with virtue, in themselves; but the inner disposition of the subject is lacking, that is, knowledge and decision, which place man above any kind of animal whatsoever.'

This perhaps might be said; but the question must be more closely examined.

Let us go back to an old problem of ascetics,[2] which today still divides mankind into two different spiritual types.

Firstly, there are some men who are continually fighting bitter inward battles, and who conquer the land of virtue, inch by inch. They know full well the meaning of inner struggle and of sacrifice. The necessary requirements for a recognition of the good life, to which they have constantly to redirect their attention, and the conscious determination to follow it, which in their case has to be renewed so often, recall the characteristic picture of virtue as described by Aristotle.

Secondly, there are on the other hand men who act with the spontaneity of children. They hardly ever stop to decide, in the common meaning of the word. For their minds conform to goodness with such responsiveness and spontaneity, that it seems—and it is partly so—that they turn instinctively towards virtue. Struggle and sacrifice to attain goodness are almost unknown to them, or else the appeal that goodness has for them is such as to make any sacrifice almost unnoticed.

---

[1] *Nichomachean Ethics*, II, 6.
[2] The science of spiritual perfection.

Now this is no easy problem: which of these two categories of men reaches the higher degree of virtue? Which is the most to be admired?

Ascetics replies: great is the merit of the inner struggle and the triumph, and the palm of victory awaits these brave warriors. But perfect virtue, as perfect art, is that which is already possessed without effort, and which is revealed as a light shining spontaneously from the whole of the being.

This culmination of serene possession of virtue is attained, according to Aristotle, through continued perseverance in actions which create the habit of virtue.

However, man could not acquire the habit of virtue, *if he were not originally capable of it*. In fact, *virtue is not entirely a habit to be acquired*. It is the attainment of a state to which we are called, just as the growth of a tree in all its luxuriance is already virtually contained in the seed.

This truth is clearly demonstrated in certain privileged spirits, of whom we may almost say that virtue is more a natural gift than a heroic and intelligent triumph (if indeed the one thing does not in an absolute sense exclude the other).

These spirits are by nature already *directed towards goodness*. They are a rare example of what man ought to have been, according to his inmost nature. In their case the distinction between thought and decision is hardly realized; both are generated so simultaneously and in such harmony.

And now we have reached the point where we must take a big step forward.

If there is goodness in animals—and their actions seem to indicate that there is—it is of this latter kind. On a different plane they are capable of that form of spontaneous virtue, I would say 'innate virtue': the virtue of the pure in heart, recalling the Gospel teaching.

Just as their thought, by nature intuitive, presents few

characteristics of meditation, so their actions are generated from simultaneous knowledge and decision. For this reason it is difficult to separate in animals the two moments so neatly focussed by the Aristotelian definition: meditated consciousness and voluntary decision. For these two moments are clearly distinguished, when they are not in contrast, only in those who have to strain their strength to attain virtue, not in those who are already fully and un-hesitatingly in possession of it.

All the same, falterings through indecision, pauses for meditation before determining upon an action are also sometimes to be found in animals, and I have cited some examples. These exceptions are very valuable in their significance: for they contribute to a revelation, if only faintly and diffidently, of some of the secrets of a conscious-ness, seemingly so crystal clear, yet for us so impenetrable, and so far removed from our own.

CHAPTER SIX

Animals and Their Inner Life

1. 'Our' world and 'theirs'

HAVING reached, by means of discussion, quotations and visible evidence, as close a definition as possible of the essential features of the animal soul, let us now try to find other examples, which, on the basis of knowledge acquired, will appear more significant.

We shall have to recognize that, in spite of very different natures, surprising analogies exist between man and animals. It is *as if man moved in the same world of values*; values of which some creatures are more, others less, aware; but which all cannot help but 'feel'.

In a word, so as to make our picture more complete, let us try to get still nearer to the life of animals, or more precisely, to their inner life.

2. Aesthetic sensibility

In his 'Praise of Birds' Leopardi maintains, and I believe with good reason, that a real inner life exists in birds, though it may only be feeble, unstable and childish, and therefore, from his point of view, more to be desired. He says:

'And if it is noted that when they are in love they sing better than ever, more often and for longer, it should not be thought, because of this, that they are not moved to song by other delights and joys as well as by those of love. For it is quite obvious that on a calm, clear day they sing more than

78

on a dull, unsettled one; and during storms they keep quite quiet, as they do too when experiencing any other kind of fear . . . Also they feel great joy in the abundance of green foliage, in fertile glens, clear, gleaming water, and in the beauty of the countryside. And in these things it is notable that what appears pleasant and charming to us appears so to them too; as can be seen from the inducements with which they are enticed into nets or on to lime, in the places where birds are trapped and snared . . . Some say, and it would be to the point to mention this here, that the voice of birds is more tender and sweeter, and their song more harmonious, in our part of the world than in those parts where men are more savage and uncouth; and they come to the conclusion that birds, being free agents, acquire some small measure of the civilization of those men with whose homes they are familiar.'[1]

Whether this last observation of some people is true or not with regard to birds, it is certainly very true for many animals in general; for, through being in contact with man, some even reach the point of losing certain of their own characteristics, which have been possessed by their species for thousands of years.

As birds clearly show, animals do not only take delight in things concerning their physical life, but they are capable of enjoying natural beauties disinterestedly and with an enjoyment which might be termed aesthetic. For a certain aesthetic appreciation is indeed included in the psychological make-up of animals, at least of the superior animals, of those who can best give us evidence of their sensibility.

It is common knowledge that animals are in general sensitive to music; it is quite clear that music says something to their spirit. As among men, there are of course some

[1] G. Leopardi (1798–1837), 'Elogio degli uccelli' (Praise of Birds), from 'Operette morali'. See note p. 113.

animals who are stubborn and perverse, and this is seen in certain canine exhibitions of disapproval of music.

Dogs are not generally among those who are more richly endowed as regards sensitivity to music; while it appears that music is greatly appreciated—whoever would have thought it?—by serpents. Which only goes to show that no creature is entirely deprived of light.

Wild beasts, too, are often deeply affected by music, as is shown by the playing of a concert as an experiment in the zoological gardens in New York. Here are the results:

'While the band played a *paso doble* the elephant shed enormous tears; two lions, busy devouring their meal, left their food and stood there listening; the wolves and tigers seemed to be enchanted; the bears, stags and gazelles all started to dance.

'A Strauss waltz, which was played immediately afterwards, nearly sent them all to sleep; Chopin's "Funeral March" brought forth a chorus of mournful wails; a jig, on the other hand, calmed them down again.

'After the concert the bears, the stags and the gazelles all went on dancing, while the lions and tigers began to howl, as they moved up and down their cages.'[1]

These examples will suffice as regards music created by man. But animals themselves are not lacking in the divine gift of inspiration. The songs of birds, the melody of the nightingale, which so deeply stirs the human soul, are the outpourings of a soul as well as a real manifestation of creative genius.

Here I should have liked to appeal to critics; but the creations of winged creatures have not yet found a place in the temple of the Muses. Poets' appreciation has been more prompt and keen; and we shall later have occasion to look at Keats's 'Ode to a Nightingale' and to Shelley's 'To a Skylark.'

[1] *Il nostro tempo*, 26th March, 1950.

3. *Love, courtship and honeymoons*

And what can be said about love in animals? This love, which is so often treated as of no importance or sneered at, can offer instances of admirable traits of beauty, faithfulness and sensitiveness; all characteristics of true love founded on feeling.

Love in animals can also be expressed *only* in feeling, as happens in human beings. Tesio, a breeder of horses, relates how two horses loved each other for the whole of their lives, and yet did little more than simply look at one another, without ever having even one little foal.

Extraordinary instances of self-sacrifice for love are to be found among fishes.

'The male salmon is completely faithful to his mate; and she will not accept any other husband unless she becomes a widow. The strange cephalopter, a flat fish with its head decorated with two queer-looking tentacles, and which sometimes weighs as much as four hundredweight, is monogamous to an excessive degree. There is a story told of how a male fish swam round and round the net in which its mate had been caught for two whole days; and on the third day it was found dead in the very same part of the net where its wife had been made prisoner.'[1]

Fishes take their love affairs very seriously indeed. There is a recent report of a sword-fish which kept following closely behind the boat on which his mate had been caught, instead of escaping to save himself; and, having given up all hope of rescuing her, he later threw himself on to the beach and let himself die beside her.

Alessandro Canestrini, in his interesting *Vita amorosa*

---

[1] Pietro Parenzan, *Oggi*, 23rd April, 1953, '*L'amore tra i pesci*' (Love among the fishes).

F

degli animali ('The Love Life of Animals'), relates how a steamer crowded with tourists cast anchor one day near an island, because they had discovered that there were sea-lions on its shores. And all those people, eager for any kind of amusement, disembarked solely for the sadistic pleasure of making a massacre of these innocent finned creatures. With guns, clubs and stones, the heroic pleasure-cruising brutes (Canestrini does not name their nationality) spent quite a while giving vent to bestial savagery against the poor defenceless living things. It was all indescribably revolting! A naturalist, who happened to be there among these human devils, and forced to witness a scene which he was powerless to prevent, noticed that one large male sea-lion refused to move in spite of the terrible rain of blows that pounded down on him. Going up to it he found that it was shielding its mate, already dead; and on the dead mother a tiny little one was staggering, completely soaked in its mother's blood . . .[1]

Storks and swallows are also among creatures who keep faith to one mate. Concerning swallows, the article just quoted has this to say:

'It should be noted that the love of swallows is an impulse so full of vigour that it does not come to an end with the act of generation in the spring. If one of the pair happens to die, it is very rare indeed that the one left, be it male or female, will get itself another mate. And this is the reason why males and females are found singly in many nests, living a life of inconsolable loneliness.'

Dogs and cats, it is well known, are much more inconstant. But there are exceptions. I once had a little female kitten, the only offspring of a faithful couple. It was given to me when barely a month old. I did not want to take it then,

---

[1] Guglielmo Bonuzzi, *L'idea Zoofila*, May, 1953, '*Bellezze e canti non sono privilegi dell 'uomo*' (Beauty and song are not only the prerogatives of man).

thinking that its mother would suffer by being deprived of it; but its mistress, for reasons of her own, was obdurate and it was not possible to send it back.

I later asked news of the mother, and I was told that she had lain quite still, without moving, for a week, because of grief. And her 'husband' had the whole time done nothing else but stay close beside her, to give her comfort. The kitten with us, for its part, mewed and cried for days on end; it was quite clear that, in spite of all our kindness and caresses, it felt quite lost without its mother.

I have also known of another faithful couple: a cat living in a certain house and 'married' to a tom, who was, unfortunately, very 'ill-mannered' (or so he was dubbed by the household), and he fled from human society and lived in the cellar. These two regularly had their kittens; and every day for years the faithful little wife took food into the cellar for her 'husband'. It was fate which finally separated them. When the family that kept the female cat moved to the country, they took her with them; and the poor tom ended by being put away.

Elephants too, and in general all wild animals, have a very keen family sense. In this connection an amusing paragraph on the 'seriousness' of elephants appeared in the magazine *Tempo*.[1]

'Male elephants pay court to their females several weeks before declaring themselves; and a female elephant cannot accept any courtship until she has reached the age of twenty. When the wedding has taken place, the male becomes the most attentive and demonstrative of mates. He is absolutely faithful and never leaves his wife except for the last months of the gestation period, and more out of a sense of respect than for any other reason. During this time the wife chooses a female friend to keep her company during her husband's

[1] 22nd September, 1951.

absence. When he reaches the age of sixty the male leaves all his fanciful notions of love behind him, and starts life again, alone and sad, but it is a solitude cheered and enlivened by sweet memories.'

With the exception of dogs, usually easily persuaded in these matters, courtship among animals is not just something of no account.[1] When two cats meet to mate for the first time, almost two whole days of coaxing, chasing, making approaches, scratching to keep him off, are needed before the courted one gives in. She-cats are not innocent like she-elephants; but they defend themselves, if only to keep up appearances.

Among fishes and birds something more is required, and that is the paying of homage, often in most sensitive and moving ways. First of all, by singing. Birds, as also crickets, sing first and foremost to touch the heart of their loved one. Then there are dances, some charming evolutions, and also actually real wedding gifts.

'The fish of paradise, a Chinese fresh-water fish, when in a frenzy of love, trembles like the cock courting the hen; and then with his mouth he takes hold of his dear one's lower lip, and thus holding her, he goes round and round her, in a prolonged kiss which sometimes may even end in tearing the skin.'[2]

Alan Devoe writes as follows:

'Even inferior creatures, when courting, go to the point of offering presents to those they love. Let us take for example the common little midges that we see flying about in swarms in the sultry air in summer, the empidae, as entomologists call them. When the male is in love, he puts

[1] For their own practical ends, men have now for centuries compelled bulls and cows to copulate most brutally. But if we consider this carefully, we shall realize that we do these poor beasts a grave injustice, in depriving them of the feeling and poetry that love spreads through all creation.

[2] P. Parenzan, art. cit.

together some dainty morsels and wraps them up in a bubble of silk, which shines brightly like quicksilver; and he offers them to the mate of his desire with the very ancient gesture of the lover, faint with emotion, as he offers his box of sweets. Some empidae express their love with even more refined gifts, such as "jewels", in the shape of a sparkling grain of sand, or of a very brightly coloured feather, or of the petal of a flower.

'Such kinds of courtship are found up and down the whole zoological scale. The crab waves his brightly coloured claws and dances in honour of his lady. Many male spiders express their love by complicated turns and pirouettes. The scorpion stretches out his "hands" and takes in his the smaller ones of his mate, and, walking backwards, takes her for a stroll. Songs of love are by no means reserved for men. When in love the crayfish croaks forth a short serenade by rubbing its feelers against its mouth, and even lobsters in love clap their claws together.

'The adélie penguins in the Antarctic have not much choice of presents in their desolate land. But the male searches among the stones and pebbles, until he finds a nice smooth polished one. Then full of hope he waddles up to his lady and lays this humble treasure at her feet.'

An exotic species of sparrow makes love by offering cherries or some such small fruit. The male puts the cherry into the female's beak, and sometimes more than one at once. If the female is won over, she accepts the fruit; but she does not eat it, instead she puts it back into her suitor's beak. The two little birds sit side by side on a branch and keep on passing gently to and fro their gift of love.

Certain birds of paradise make Nature's most lovely gifts to plight their troth. The male constructs a complicated little 'cottage', sometimes two yards high or more and up to four and a half yards long, and he decorates it beautifully with berries and brightly coloured flowers. Into this he invites the lady of his heart. The silky-feathered female bird of paradise has blue eyes, and so her lover brings her gifts of wild blue berries, blue stones and other little things of this kind, all blue in colour to match her eyes.

Like Our Lady's Tumbler, males of the animal world often know no better way of expressing their love than by feats of prowess. The humming-bird's ethereal display is, for instance, quite breath-taking. With wings quivering he goes back and forth through the air, in front of the female, describing arcs like those of a pendulum; backwards and forwards, up and down, with wings beating a rhythm of seventy-five strokes a second. As more and more passionately he performs his silent love-poem, so his arc of flight reaches higher and higher, higher and higher until, suddenly, the little winged creature, pointing straight up towards heaven, shoots upward like an arrow from a bow, going about twenty yards into space. For a moment he hovers there, up on high. Then straight down he drops to earth in a joyful and rapturous descent which stops, miraculously, in mid-air, just when he is on a level with the female, watching him from her perch among the leaves. There he stays poised facing her, hovering on his quivering wings and sparkling like a gorgeous jewel.

Ardent love expressed by courtship and by union is not, however, the only kind of mutual affection existing among Nature's creatures. In their lives, as in human life, we find the calm and constant joy of living together; there is tenderness, faithfulness and devotion even to death.

'In the northern Canadian forests one of the most well-known non-professional naturalists is an ex-trapper called Long Joe. He tells how one day a female bear was caught in his trap, and when he arrived on the scene the she-bear's mate was there too, and the great shaggy beast was embracing his mate, holding her tightly and sobbing aloud.

'Wolves and foxes live in couples until they die, and all dog-lovers know that the same devotion may be found in the canine species. A year or two ago, for example, a bitch, of no particular breed, fell down a crevice. Her loyal husband and lover was a setter, he, too, no great beauty. During the ten days that passed before the search party could get to the bitch, the setter saved his mate from dying of hunger, by eating only a few bites of his own meal each evening and carrying off the rest to throw down to her in the crevice.

'The canine world is also full of stories of faithful love. Darby and Joan were two Belgian sheep dogs who together went through the period of the air-raids on London. When the warning sounded, Joan used to run whining to her bed and crouch down on it. Darby, wherever he was at the time, used to rush home and throw himself on top of his trembling mate and defend her with his body. The two dogs were lying in this position when the first-aid squad dug them out after their house had collapsed in a raid. Joan was safe because Darby's large black body, now cold and stiff in death, had taken the full force of the explosion.'

It is easy to fall into the danger of too much sentiment in one's attitude towards animals, and to attribute to their actions human thoughts and feelings, which is quite wrong. But it is just as easy to make the opposite mistake, and to forget that there is a sense of brotherhood in the whole of creation, and that in the heart and mind of any being thoughts and feelings exist which are common to us all.

'When dealing with ornithology the term "honeymoon" might seem to be much too romantic. But the most serious scientists have come to the conclusion that this is the correct expression when studying herons. Flocks of herons arrive in Louisiana, after wintering in places in South America, and they then go off in pairs, each pair choosing a place to build a nest, and then they withdraw into it. But they do not set about having a family right away. There is first a honeymoon, with such characteristics of passionate tenderness and devotion, that when the English scientist, Julian Huxley, saw it for the first time, he could not believe that it was the normal thing in the life of these birds.

'For some days the two herons are always together, perched for hours without moving, the female on a branch a little below the one on which the male is perched, and she leans her head against his side. Every now and then, when calm happiness changes to ecstasy, both herons open their wings and stretch out their long necks; and then, breaking into loving cries, they twine their necks together. A heron's neck is long and supple enough to go completely once round another's neck; and so the birds entwine themselves together in a true lovers' knot.

'Then each bird seizes its companion's beautiful feathers in its beak (the famous 'aigrettes' or tufts) and lovingly nibbles them, 'kissing' each feather from its base to its point. When this ecstasy of love is ended, the two herons untie their necks and fall again into the mood of quiet happiness, side by side. The honeymoon often lasts for four or five days.'[1]

4. *Offspring; family sense*

At this point I feel almost tempted to conclude my study. In fact, what is the good of so labouring the point, with examples and philosophical conclusions, in order to demonstrate a spiritual quality that has already given such eloquent proof of its existence?

But not wishing to fall short of the aim I have set myself,

[1] *Reader's Digest,* February, 1951, 'Animals in Love'.

I will continue and we will now turn to a study of family sense in animals. Creatures who feel the emotion of love to such a point as we have seen will not disappoint us when it comes to a question of tenderness to offspring. This is a topic which is both moving and melancholy, for almost always the inflexibility of natural law must take the upper hand and after the tender family tie comes the inevitable separation.

However, it cannot be denied that if circumstances are favourable there is a continuance of maternal care among animals, and of this I have collected the following examples.

In a small village, a far-sighted little bitch 'placed' her son in the house of a friend of mine, sure that he would be well treated there. After she had left him, she went to see him periodically, and she caressed him and played with him; but when she had to come away she was quite unmoved by the whining of her puppy. That was the house suited to him and there he had to stay. As time went on, her visits became less and less frequent, until they stopped altogether. Yet for many years afterwards, whenever mother and son met in the village, they made such a very special fuss that it really seemed as if they recognized each other.

And I have heard of the following incident, which is really most remarkable, from the mistress of two female cats, mother and daughter, who lived together. When the daughter was going to have kittens the mother began to follow her about everywhere. When they were born, the grandmother brought the kittens one by one to the mother to be fed and then she took them away again, so that her daughter could have her rest.

My own cat once had a 'big' daughter of seven months old and a little kitten of only a month. Her affection for both of them was shown with extraordinary impartiality. The little one was still being suckled; but otherwise there was no difference at all in their treatment: the same care, the same conscientious washing were given to both. And the young grown-up cat, nearly as big as her mother, showed how much she felt that she was a 'daughter'.

Whoever would have imagined that baby hippopotamuses are so attached to their parents that if they are captured by themselves they have to have a man with them for weeks on end, for the sole object of comforting them?

And this is what Dr. Chierichetti relates, in his *Le Bestie Hanno un' Anima*, about two little birds: when he was at Gimma in the Galla-Sidamo region, a native brought him a baby bird, a weaver bird, which he reared with very great care. Almost immediately the mother of the bird came to help him, for, having tracked down her little one, she began to come each day to feed it. When the little one was ready to fly, this is what happened:

'One morning I came out of my tent,' writes the doctor, 'and I put the cage in its usual place and set off to my work. But all along the path I was pursued, I could almost say, both on the ground and in the air by a little bird, and I could not understand what it was all about. With shrill little cries and often landing on the ground in front of my feet or almost flying in my face, this little bird tried to stop me going on my way. So I stood still where I could observe it, at that moment perched on a low branch in front of me. And I saw that it was the mother of my little prisoner, the one whom I used to see coming to feed him every morning. How often words are less expressive than such humble silence! I turned back, and while I went nearer to my tent, the bird's flight came closer and closer to my face, and the shrill cries grew louder as if asking for something, joyously and boisterously. I opened the little door of the cage and the prisoner came out. He went straight to his mother, and the two of them rose, singing together, towards the sun, pouring forth at the kiss of its golden light a wonderful hymn of freedom and of joy.'

In this case, the wise little mother had not given up hope. In many cases, however, it is known that when birds find their offspring imprisoned, they prefer to poison them.

Here we touch on a problem both difficult and arresting: that of mothers who abandon their offspring if they cannot feed them or if they find that they are afflicted with some serious infirmity.

I know of a cat who gave birth to seven kittens, and as she was not able to feed them all, she took away two of them and left them a long way off, so that the rest could be suckled properly; and of a bitch who, after having begun to suckle her pup, one day suddenly left it. It was then found that the puppy had had a dislocated hip from birth, and so bad a form of dislocation that even the veterinary surgeon would not consent to try and cure it, although the pup was a thoroughbred.

Do these mothers who subordinate feeling to reason in this truly amazing way suffer because of it? It might be supposed that they do. But they prefer to decide in time, rather than bring up creatures not strong enough to face life's challenge.

This is a dangerous subject; for some might think that the same treatment could be allowed and might be right for human beings. But with the far greater possibilities of the human spirit, we can make of life a thing of so much greater value than can the animals. And besides, we are capable of curing our little ones who are ill, of providing them with the aid of science and technical skill. But not so the animals; they are more limited by the inflexible law of nature. For them it is right not to bring up a little one, to which later they will not be able to give the necessary aid.

*   *   *

And how does the father behave? Among wild animals the father usually plays a very loving and active part in the family. He gets food for his wife and children, and he teaches these latter what they need to know before going out into their world. Among some fishes, as for example the sea-horse, it is the mother who is relieved of all care and anxiety, for she leaves the eggs to be looked after by her husband, and even to be hatched by him, in his ventral pouch. Also among some other fishes the males have the duty of making the nest and of protecting the birth of their offspring.

On the other hand, among domestic animals the father usually knows nothing at all about his own children; he is not even acquainted with them. But this is man's fault, more than anything else, for it is he who separates the members of a family. In fact, in favourable circumstances we even find among some animals complete characteristics of wedded life. For instance I know of a tom-cat who used to look after the kittens while his wife, their mother, had a well-earned rest; and of another who, when his wife was absent, used to stretch himself over the basket to keep their kittens warm. For fathers, we all know, do what they can, when they think they ought to be making themselves useful.

In contrast to this idyllic picture there are examples of just the opposite, fortunately rather rare: scenes of jealousy, males betrayed by their mate who kill the children of the faithless one; examples all the more impressive because of their similarity with the most terrible of human passions. And there are instances, though again quite rare, of mothers who will have nothing to do with their own children.

*   *   *

Finally we must mention a custom common among

animals, which reveals an advanced stage of development of the maternal instinct, and that is: *adoption*.

'Among herds of wild horses, if a mother happens to die, other mares will rear the little foal; and Aristotle himself informs us that some mares who have no young have been known to persuade the little foals of others to follow them, with very moving gestures; and they have shown great tenderness and given careful protection to their adopted children.'[1]

But we can go further. The sense of solidarity among animals is such that they will adopt offspring of quite a different species.

The curious fact of a cat adopting chickens has been noted more than once. Less frequent, but possible, is a case of the other way round. An example is to be found in a French psychological review of last September. A hen, who had abandoned her nest after having brooded over her eggs all in vain, became fond of four little kittens just born to a cat. One day, while the cat had gone off in search of food, the hen got into the basket and gathered the kittens under her wings. For some time there was a real struggle between the cat and the hen; and it was only after fierce battling that the cat was at length able to suckle her own kittens. At last, however, the cat got tired of all the bother and went off, leaving the hen mistress of the field. The results of the hen's rearing of the kittens were obviously quite disastrous; for she stupidly insisted on teaching the kittens to peck up grain, and she got annoyed if they did not follow her, as she walked up and down, like chickens generally do . . .[2]

Hens are notoriously sentimental; but common sense is not one of their strong points.

---

[1] *L'Idea Zoofila*, May, 1953. G. Bonuzzi, art. cit.
[2] Giorgio Assan, '*La scienza illustrata*', August, 1953, '*Qualità umane degli animali*' (Human characteristics in animals).

'Stranger still,' continues the writer of this article, 'are cases of adoption between species of animals who are by nature enemies. Romanes, the naturalist, relates how, when the mother of three little ferrets died, he gave these orphans into the care of a hen, who had been brooding eggs for about a month without result: and the hen adopted the ferrets and kept them with her for two weeks.'

In spite of the proverbial enmity between dogs and cats, there are cases here too, and not infrequent, of mutual help. Here is a case which, although already quoted in various works on animal psychology, we give again because of some of its curious features. A spaniel bitch had given birth to five puppies, and as she was not strong enough to feed them all, two were taken from her and given to a she-cat in place of her kittens which had all been born dead. The cat brought up the two puppies with the greatest care, and at the end of a fortnight her two pups were much more advanced than the three that had stayed with the real mother. While these three still wobbled about and rolled rather than walked, the other two were quick and nimble, just like kittens. When the two adopted children were taken from the cat, she was quite inconsolable, and for two days she did nothing but go restlessly all round the house in a desperate effort to find them. At last she succeeded in entering the room where the spaniel was nursing the three pups that had been left with her; and she must have thought that the dog had stolen her two children. There was a fearful battle, and the cat was victorious. She took off one of the pups in her teeth and hid it in a safe place, and then returned to the charge. After a second battle she succeeded in carrying away another. She left the third with the rightful mother. The clever animal confined her efforts to recovering the two puppies that had been taken from her, showing among other things that animals also have a sense of *numbers*.

The sight of motherhood among animals rouses in us a strange emotion. Perhaps because of their innocence, which is so appealing, the sight of a kitten or a baby lion or a baby rabbit holding tightly to its mother touches us deep down in the depths of our soul.

It is not a question of whether one is an animal-lover or not. It is a question of recognizing one of the clearest notes of the universe. If animals inspire a deep respect, it is because of that aura of integrity, of 'spiritual' intangibility which surrounds them. Their fundamental innocence, as has been said, is not simply negative, it is a fact of the 'soul'.

*   *   *

One of the greatest sorrows that man inflicts on animals without caring is that caused by the snatching away of the little ones from their mothers. If he thought for a moment how cruel this act is, he would at least be worried by it, even though powerless to prevent it.

Fortunately for them, animals are a bit like children, who cry bitterly and then forget easily. But this does not mean that their grief is any the less keenly felt. And later if they seem to have got over it, what do we really know about their capacity to forget? One example may be sufficient as an indication: that of a heroine, a cat in Buenos Aires, who, when her kittens were taken from her, defiant and mad with grief, took refuge up a tree and stayed there *for three years* without once coming down. People living near, touched by her sorrow, fed her up there, and it may be that she is there still.

What is to be done then? Shall the little ones be left with the mother indefinitely? No, but the moment of separation should be put off as long as possible; and all the little ones should not be taken away at the same time, but one by one;

and the last one should be left with her until it simply has to be given away. Kittens ought to be left with their mother and their brothers for at the very least two months, better still for three months or three and a half, and even for longer. It will be seen how they fondle each other and how happily they play together. I am sorry that I have to write these lines, that is, to bring 'numbers' into the sanctuary of motherhood, for such it is also for animals, as for human beings. But, compelled by the necessities of life, we have to choose the lesser evil.

Some people put down the whole litter of kittens, especially of cats that are very prolific. And if one thinks of the future of such cats, this is perhaps providential, if sad. But *all* the little ones should not be done away with at once; it is easy to realize how cruel this is for the poor mother. Nor should she be left with only one. Kittens and puppies need at least one little brother to play with, that is part of their childhood. Have you never noticed how much more grave, I would say even melancholy, puppies are without brothers? We should not deprive animals of the fundamental joys of life.

Finally a suggestion for the time when animals have to be separated, big and small, and even those who are only just friends. They should be allowed to say goodbye to one another. This is *important*. I have often experienced it. If you take the little one to the mother to kiss and then tell her that it is *going away* (this sounds very childish, but animals understand our words much better than we think), when she sees it go out of the door of the house in a basket, her grief will be calmed. For she will not suffer the anguish of *not being able to find it any more*, and the plucky little creature will be reasonable and will end by becoming resigned to her loss without much difficulty.

In fact one of the most painful kinds of mental suffering

endured by animals is that caused by the unknown. When they leave each other and when they separate, they are given into the care of other people, and they do not know whether it is for always or not. They leave the house where they have been born; will they ever come back? One can imagine how their little heads are worried by questions to which they have no answer. Who bothers to give them any *explanations?* Their son, or their friend, or the one they always played with so much has suddenly vanished. Perhaps he is dead? They look for him, they call him; there is no reply.

Let us try then to talk to them, to calm them; for in the great majority of cases they will understand us.

5. *The prerogatives of the heart*

Of the various kinds of violence done to animals, castration is without a doubt one of the most odious. It not only does harm to the creature physically, but it causes irreparable damage to its character.

Better death for a proud cock, full of vitality, than to be transformed into a fat capon, which is half stupefied. The addition of a few extra ounces of flesh certainly does not justify this infamy on the part of a vulgar, greedy mankind. Human beings ought to realize this.

Other animals subjected to this abuse, not because of greed, but through their owner's short-sighted affection for them, are cats. As superior animals, they feel the effects of it less in their mental integrity. But think of the nervous upset, the lowering of the 'tone' of their lives which comes from it just the same. Poor enormous pussies, they are still affectionate and intelligent, but they lack something which can never be replaced. Perhaps they no longer feel any sexual desire (or at least not fully; but this, too, has still to

G

be proved), but they are deprived of love. We humans show a great lack of imagination about what animals may feel. And all this is done to protect them from the consequences of their own vitality; as if life is not given to be lived intensely, for all it has to give, even at the cost of being short.

There is, however, one way to find a cure for the dangerous consequences of love, the most simple and the traditional one: marriage.

It is hardly believable how the boldest of males make most affectionate mates. My own Persian cat had a very stormy married life at first. The she-cat would not look at him, so he took to the roof, much to the anxiety of all the family. But later she changed her mind and he never tried to run away again. When his wife was going to have kittens, he surrounded her with affection and kindness; and when they were born, he acted as midwife. Now they both sleep together in their basket with the kittens in the middle, and 'daddy' helps to wash them, look after and protect them. This is not to be wondered at; for cats are the descendants of the large feline species, and it is a well-known fact that lions and tigers live an exemplary family life.

But what has been said goes for all animals in general. Cats, canaries, little fishes (and it is cruel to keep these in small tanks)—no domestic animals ought to be kept in solitude. Love, family, matrimony, these are the natural joys of life, which we do not deny ourselves, and which we have no right to deny the animals.

6. Sense of ownership

Animals have not yet penned a code of civil rights, but, contrary to what used to be thought, they are not lacking in sense of ownership. We now know that birds sing to define the boundaries of their territory; and that wild beasts who are shut up in the zoo are not all that unhappy, because having an enclosure of their own, where they feel they are masters, compensates to some degree for the freedom which they have lost.

There certainly exists a kind of pitiless communism in some of the amazing social organizations, as among bees and ants, and above all among the termites, where it reaches a technical perfection and an inexorable inflexibility. But even members of such societies have, if nothing else, their *own* hive, their *own* anthill, their *own* city, and each individual its duty.

But among other animals there is indeed a sense of ownership, a sense that I would call 'sentimental'. Each one has its house, its den, its family.

A noteworthy example is that of the two beetles, already mentioned, where one was the lawful owner, to whom even a place of honour was due, while the other was simply an assistant. We have also seen what extraordinary wedding gifts penguins, birds of paradise, and midges offer to their loved ones. On the other hand, I know of a cat couple who did not see eye to eye in the matter of generosity. 'Outside' they loved each other very much and got on very well together. But woe betide if either had the impudence to go into the house of the other! Love is all right, but . . . rights are rights, and the home is exclusive property and not to be touched, at least for these two.

And ownership inside the home? Those who possess only few objects for their own personal use are known to become very fond of the least attractive of things. Toto, the dog, was very fond indeed of his lead (his 'rope' as Grandfather used to say). He used to stand guard over it and, so that he could sleep soundly at night, it had to be put close by him on the armchair.

A little cat, Geppina, had found a hiding place for her toys, and she used to put them away there most conscientiously. And what shall we say about the wonderful presents that dogs make to their masters as a sign of special good-will, when they come bounding in, all triumphant, to lay at their feet the most odd array of objects?

Dr. Chierichetti[1] relates a curious story about Gamine, a pomeranian, who after a period of ten months, when the family went back to their country home, insisted on fetching from its hiding place the ball she had put there.

'When you arrive at night after a long journey, besides being tired there is the feeling that things are all over the place, so that you would much rather put off till the next day the unpacking and settling in; all you want is a good meal and a restful bed.

'But Gamine, unlike her three companions who were eager for food, began to bark, giving little short yelps just in front of the door leading to the wooden staircase which goes to the upper floor. And she kept scratching with her claws to open it and simply would not leave it. So at last it was opened for her, and with a great bound she rushed upstairs to one of the upper rooms and after a few moments we heard regular thuds on the steps of the staircase, and then there appeared Gamine with her favourite wooden ball, which was to be her toy for the whole of our stay in the country.'

In conclusion we may say that animals are moderate and law-abiding as regards ownership, as they are in general regarding most affairs in this world (and possibly even as regards those in the next, as we are trying to demonstrate).

7. *Sense of humour; games*

Another aspect of the life of animals which should not be

[1] *Op. cit.*

left out of consideration, for it denotes a certain detachment from practical life, is a sense of humour, for traces of a sense of humour can be detected in animals: parrots for instance when they keep repeating phrases which are *to the point* seem to be making fun, not only of others, but also of themselves.

One day behind our cottage in the country there was a noble assembly of cats. There was the big black tom, the Persian she-cat from town with a ribbon round its neck (who had completely captivated Fido, not used to such elegance) and the little grey cat that never grew any bigger.

Up comes jolly fellow Fido, bursting with youthful high spirits (he is not much more than a puppy) and he playfully begins to tease the cats. He chases the black cat, but the tom runs off and then comes back for more; he tries to rouse the she-cat, she replies playfully, but stands her ground. Finally he gently rolls the little cat about with his paws, as if it were a ball; and the cat, the plucky little thing, is not a bit frightened nor does it try to run away, but shows that it appreciates the fun. Fido laughed. He *did* laugh! There was positively no doubt about it. A sign of the superiority of the canine world is just this: a dog knows how to laugh.

Now a story about a dog called Pupi, another jolly sort too, but a very different character indeed in its psychological complexity. To give a true idea of his personality one would need to research into many fields. An unusual amount of self-conceit was at the bottom of all his cunning.

It will suffice to say that at dinner time he required a special personal invitation to the table. He took up his place on a chair near the door and with great dignity watched the whole family troop in. Why in the world were they so long in inviting *him*? Pupi was hungry, but he did not come down from his pedestal. Time passed, so he began to bark, louder and louder. When the family could bear it no longer, someone went up to him to invite him officially. You had to say: 'Pupi, dinner is ready.' Only then would he come down from his chair satisfied.

But do not think that that was the end of it. Was it because his mistress was soft, or because Pupi was a bully? Pupi 'agreed' to take his soup, but only if it were given him in a spoon. And things did not end there. Either through naughtiness or wanting to pose he pretended at first that he did not want it; and when the spoon was held near his mouth, he turned his head majestically away, but taking care to roll his eyes back again, with a crafty look, to be sure that the spoon was not taken away. The spoon was just going to move away from him; so then he made a slight movement of his head towards it, so that it would not go too far off. But it was still too soon for him to decide to take it. Immediately he turned his head away again, but not so far this time, and always looking out of the corner of his eye. So a kind of swaying of a pendulum began, with its oscillations getting shorter and shorter, until at last Pupi condescended to accept the first spoonful, after which all the others were swallowed right heartily.

But all kinds of other complications could arise to make dinner late. Even of an aesthetic order, for example. One day they bought Pupi an earthenware basin, of the good old style, specially made for dogs. A grave mistake. Pupi looked down his nose at it haughtily and refused to eat out of it. We had to give in and pour his soup into the usual white saucer, much more civilized. Only then would he be satisfied.

Such was Pupi, the most complex character of a dog that I have ever known, and one to confound all the firmest convictions of philosophers with regard to animals.

What can we say about wild animals and their desire for amusement?

Alan Devoe, the famous naturalist, can help here. He relates:

'A grey bear can seem to be a terrifying beast if you see his great bulk come charging at your pistol point; but he is a beast who finds tremendous fun at playing at sliding down an incline in the snow. He will climb up time and time again to the top of a steep snowy slope for the fun of slithering down just like a little boy playing at toboganing.

'Even a small hippopotamus, born in an Amsterdam zoo, found a way of playing all by itself. One day a maple leaf fell into its pool. The hippopotamus slid its great hulk gently into the pool and swam underneath the floating leaf. Then it puffed out a light breath with its nostrils and sent the leaf flying into the air. When the leaf fell in again, the animal gave another puff into the air, and for many hours the great beast played all by itself at "leaf" completely absorbed in the delight of the game.

'There is no animal in the woods duller than the porcupine; but even porcupines play at having a fight, and succeed in not pricking each other, goodness only knows how. Giving blows with their dreadful prickly tails does not count, however keen the battle wages.

'Animals in herds together play at games which are surprisingly like those of children. When a roe-buck who is "it" tries to catch another, it makes an effort to "tick" it properly, touching it with its hoof. Many roe-bucks play a sort of mixture of "tick" and "hide and seek". They all separate, and then look for each other very cautiously around a hillock, and the game consists in seeing which roe-buck manages to "get home" most cleverly, without being seen, and deceiving those after it. The practice acquired in these games has obviously saved the lives of many roe-bucks.

'For young animals playing is the school to fit them for

life; but grown animals also enjoy games like young ones. Old grey otters let themselves slip down from their muddy beaches with the same joy as their little ones. In the gopher colonies in the American prairies in the West these rodents play for hours at their own version of "puss in the corner". One gopher runs to the den of another; a third tries to get to the first one's den before he can get back. And the game spreads until the whole colony is in commotion. They run around, collide with each other, think up plans to obstruct one another. And their little squeals and squeaks are as excited as the shouting at a football match.

'Even elephants play games. The African explorer, Carl Akeley, once went very cautiously up to a herd of elephants in a forest. These huge thick-skinned beasts were going about stamping their feet; but they did not appear to be either afraid or angry. So he went nearer still. When finally he got near enough to them to see them properly he stood there open-mouthed. For the elephants had a ball of soil, hardened in the sun, about the size of half a yard in diameter. And there under the eyes of Akeley, they rolled it forward, pushing it along with their trunks and their feet for the distance of nearly a mile along the green paths of the forest.'[1]

8. Compassion; attitude to death

Many animals feel compassion. It is unnecessary to insist on this point after all that has been said on their goodness in general; but this tender aspect of their sensibility ought to be emphasized.

It is sufficient to recall the incident of the rat who was leading his blind companion with a piece of straw, or the

[1] *Reader's Digest*, November, 1950.

grown-up cat that kept to one side to let the smaller one feed first (a very frequent case indeed), or of the mothers who adopt orphans.

Another example may be quoted from the cat exhibition at Turin in 1953 where a cat called Pucci attracted general attention; in fact, he was mentioned in the newspapers for his extraordinary work as a benefactor. For when he found a famished cat in the road he used to invite it to his home, and there he mewed until the plate had been filled for his guest (a thing he never did at all when he wanted food himself). When the other cat had had enough, he immediately escorted it to the door (charity is all right, but there's no need to risk one's own rights) and there, kindly but firmly, he bade it goodbye.

And Giorgio Assan quotes a very interesting case of 'protection' afforded to an unlucky creature:

'A cock whose feet were almost paralysed by rheumatism was continually ill-treated by its companions in the hen-run; and it had the lucky notion of taking refuge from their attacks near to an old dog, a setter bitch. Those that were after the cock made to attack it even there, but the dog, annoyed by all the bother, soon chased them off. From then on the disabled cock seemed to understand perfectly that it was the object of this protection, for from that day it made its home beneath the dog's kennel, a kennel that was raised up on four short legs. It stayed there and kept putting out its beak and darting glances upwards, which seemed to be looks of gratitude directed towards its protector, who was resting just above it. And the dog allowed the cock to peck in her basin, when her food was brought, and she always left a little bread in it, while the other animals in the yard were never allowed to take such liberties. One rainy day, when the basin had been put inside the kennel, the dog, after she had eaten enough, threw what remained of her meal on to the ground, so that her unfortunate companion could eat too. And every time afterwards when her food was given her in her kennel, after she had had hers, she never failed to perform this act of charity towards the poor lame cock. Sometimes she pushed the basin forward with her nose and tipped it outside the kennel; more often she picked up bits of bread in her mouth and dropped them on to the ground below.'[1]

* * *

What is the attitude of animals to death?

In general all animals hide when they feel they are about to die. This premonition is as gentle and resigned as the feeling of terror is keen and sharp when they feel they are threatened or pursued. Animals led to slaughter suffer much more mentally than physically, for they 'know' where they are being taken.

Not all animals hide, however, when they feel death near. Sometimes a love for someone, a desperate longing to be near to someone, can overcome their common instinct.

I once had a kitten, only two months old, who was desperately ill of an incurable disease. One evening, without realizing the gravity of her condition, I put her little basket near my bed before going to sleep. Early in the morning I woke up to find that the little creature, who the day before had never moved, had summoned up enough strength to clamber on to my bed and to come and rest, like a lifeless thing, quite close to me. She was dying. I spoke to her, even though she seemed already a long way off, and out of reach. But that was perhaps what she had wanted, as she had tried to get so near to me. A short while afterwards she died.

[1] *La scienza illustrata,* August, 1953, art. cit.

We know that monkeys, weeping and wailing, are capable of keeping their little dead one in their arms for days. And here we should recall too that sword-fish, which voluntarily threw itself on to the beach beside its dead mate; and the male sea-lion also, who, under the rain of blows, stayed to shield its dead mate and its little one.

One day I found a lost kitten and brought it home. Our she-cat and her kittens immediately took a friendly interest in it. The mother cat watched over it like her own kittens and kept it washed very conscientiously, although she refused to suckle it. But the little waif was, we discovered, very ill, and it died two days later.

I put the little body in a box, for I wanted to see what reactions there would be from the others. I called one of the kittens: "Come and see poor little pussy." The kitten did not hide a certain feeling and gave it a last little lick. The mother, of sterner stuff, passed by, but not without having also given it a rapid lick. This was a scene of only a few seconds, but quite revealing.

Even ants, creatures certainly less liable to transports of emotion, offer example of real funeral ceremonies, the whole community taking part. How much real homage or spiritual regard can there be in such a manifestation?

Dr. Chierichetti, already quoted, has something to say about this.

'Romanes refers to a story, told him by a lady who had just returned from tropical Africa, about a funeral of ants. During the ceremony, while engaged with others in carrying four of their kind who had died while at work, four of them left their posts. And immediately these four slackers were killed and transported to a kind of ditch far away from the burial place for those of them who had died without infamy or unworthiness.'[1]

[1] *Op. cit.*

Those guilty of insubordination in a communist state always come to a bad end. All the same, if this lady's story is correct, ants would appear to show a most remarkable discrimination, a real critical faculty capable of judging their own kind.

There exist too, it is true, insects who act as grave-diggers. But this is a different question. The accounts of funerals among ants, now generally accepted, present a special interest, on a moral plane. We await further observations which may tell us something more about the spirit which appears to animate this 'social act' in the face of death.

9. *Leisure*

Work, play, falling in love, looking after little ones: we cannot say that the life of animals is not a full one.

They appear to be creatures wholly dedicated to an active life. But on the other hand, there are long periods of silence and inactivity when animals are almost completely still. Their eyes are open, watchful, yet immersed in thought. Is it rest? Contemplation? Who knows? But it is something which commands respect and awe as one looks at them.

Perhaps Leopardi's 'flock',[1] which seems so happy to the nomad shepherd, has no experience of tedium because it is lulled in the gentle happiness of feeling itself alive, in a very primitive feeling of calm relaxation. And yet . . . there is something that troubles one, all the same, at the sight of the gentle sheep, calm, self-possessed and silent.

Perhaps dogs wander in their imagination, when they are quite still, dreaming; for they shake themselves every now and then, and move even when they are asleep. Their

[1] Lyric poem, '*Canto notturno di un pastore*. . . .' (Night song of a shepherd) from *I Canti* by G. Leopardi. See note p. 113.

emotional and active life must penetrate deeply into their soul.

Not so cats, who, with their pupils fixed, are yet wide awake, though as still as a sphinx. Not for nothing did the ancient Egyptians make a kind of divinity of the cat. The cat's abstraction seems almost priestly, perhaps of a nature superior to that of any other animal. But cats are not ascetics. They pass with a bound, and with wonderful sureness, from the most metaphysical immobility to immediate participation in whatever surrounds them in the world of transient things. In their feline nature they are perfect spirits. They must have a power of concentration and a gift for relaxation that man rarely experiences. It is just then, when one is trying to penetrate into their glance, that one feels more than ever to be on the threshold of an unrevealed mystery.

CHAPTER SEVEN

Supernormality in Animals

THERE is a charming legend which tells how, each Christmas eve, animals acquire the gift of speech; that is, of human speech. But this is not simply pure imagination if, as is the case during the last thirty or forty years, we have instances of animals deigning to communicate their ideas and impressions to us by means of the letters of our own alphabet. Such examples are afforded us by the dog Rolf and the little bitches Lola and Peg; and, encouraged by these, a little cat Daisy has also learnt to write.

We will not go into the case of the famous Elberfeld horses, which were capable of extracting cube roots on the spot, without previous preparation. It appears to have been proved beyond doubt that there was no deception in these exhibitions. I myself was present when the little lap-dog Peg[1] did her mathematical calculations, solving the problems put to her by perfect strangers; and after this it seems to me that it is quite out of the question to go on refusing to believe in these things.

It is possible for animals to be endowed with a faculty for mathematics, and, in certain cases, with a memory far superior to a normal human one; and it is very surprising that people can receive such evidence with a coolness and an indifference which are, to me, quite extraordinary, convinced as I am of the spiritual quality of the animal soul. There is another example too, of the little monkey, Viky, who, quite

[1] *'Il nostro tempo'*, 31st May, 1953. At the interview in the Hotel Genio, Turin, technicians from the R.A.I. (Radio Audizioni Italiane, i.e. Italian equivalent of the B.B.C.) were also present to make a recording.

contrary to all the established notions about monkeys since their species came into being, has learnt to pronounce quite distinctly the three words: 'papa', 'mamma', and 'cup'. It is just as if a magic world were opening for us; that fairy-tale world that inspired our dreams in childhood, and of which primitive peoples have always dreamed.

Still more disquieting, I would say even distressing, because of our powerlessness to explain it, is the extraction of square, cube and quarter roots, without any previous preparation. Not even the most expert mathematician could do this without some preliminary calculation. The fact that the answers are given instantly proves that they are obtained without any reckoning at all. Yet they are found to be perfectly correct.

All this would make us feel that we were going off our heads, if a faculty somewhat similar in kind had not been found elsewhere, among Indians. It is naturally of extremely rare occurrence, and is handed down through a long line of ancestry. One of them explained his ability by saying: "I see the number of the root." Is it perhaps a question of psychic powers rather than mathematical skill? In what hidden depths of the mind is the number revealed instantly as a clear entity, free from the laws of the laborious workings of the chain of thought? Perhaps in other worlds, beyond our life. At times the soul succeeds in soaring confidently aloft into those mysterious regions.

If we wished to move towards this field of study, I could cite many an example of a sure presentiment of the future in animals. For instance, our dog Pupi died after being knocked down by a car, when in the very prime of life; and three days before it happened he kept whining piteously and so insisted on being petted and comforted—a thing most unusual in him—that I was quite alarmed. Some animals 'feel' the death of their master or of one of their own kind at the very moment that it happens, though they may be many miles away; and some animals feel the presence of spirits much more keenly than do men (it is well known that spiritualist séances cannot take place when cats are in the room). Finally there are instances of animals who have appeared after death, looking so real and life-like that only later was it realized that one had been in the presence of a ghost.[1]

But I will not pursue this theme. It would mean saying too much and, at the same time, too little, and it would be allowing ourselves to be led away with this too tangible evidence from what is of more importance. Psychic phenomena will probably be able to confirm the immortality of the soul; but it will never be able to take the place of the intuition of Socrates, so highly charged with spiritual quality.

[1] Ernesto Bozzano, *Gli Animali Hanno un' Anima?*

CHAPTER EIGHT

Poets' Intuitions

LET us hear finally what poets have to say upon our subject;
for poetry reveals the true face of things by its own peculiar
gift of intuition and spontaneous insight.

We may take, for example, Leopardi's ode, '*Il passero
solitario*,'[1] where the boundless world of the human mind is
transferred with perfect analogy into the tiny soul of a bird,
the image conforming clearly and precisely with the idea.
This, as we shall see, is also a characteristic of many of the
parables of Our Lord.

> 'Thou, pensive and aloof, gaze on it all;
> no friends for thee, no flights;
> thou carest not for mirth and dost enjoyment shun;
> thou singest and in song dost leave behind
> of the year and of thy life the loveliest flower.'[2]

The bird's life ends differently from that of man, however,
according to the poet; for the little bird, unlike man, is not
saddened when it has to die:

> 'Thou, lonely little bird, when thou hast come
> to the evening of the life the stars ordained for thee;
> thy state then surely
> will not sadden thee; for fruit of nature
> is each desire of thine.'[3]

But in the same poet's '*Canto notturno d'un pastore*',[4] this

---

[1] '*Il passero solitario*' (The Rock Sparrow) from *I Canti* by Giacomo Leopardi,
1798–1837, greatest Italian lyric poet of modern times.
[2] '*Il passero solitario*', vv. 12–16; an almost literal, line-for-line translation which
is the method adopted throughout for the rendering of Italian poetry.
[3] *idem*. vv. 45–9.
[4] '*Canto notturno di un pastore. . . .*' (Night song of a shepherd), from *I Canti*,
op. cit.

113

H

cosmic anguish seems to weigh upon the whole of the universe, and to be searching for a reason for itself even from the life of the flock of sheep; for perhaps it is beginning to obtrude, like a first, thin ray of the pale light of dawn into the consciousness even of these creatures. At first, however, the shepherd thinks that this is not so:

> 'O my flock at rest, o happy thou,
> for thy wretchedness thou knowest not, or so I trow.
> How I do envy thee!
> Not only because from all anxiety
> thou art most nearly free . . .
>
> for thine every want, every pain
> every despairing fear, is straight away forgotten;
> but more because thou never feelest boredom . . .
>
> What thou enjoyest, or how much
> I do not know; but fortunate art thou . . .
>
> If thou could'st speak, I would then ask of thee:
> tell me: why, when lying
> in comfort and at ease,
> each animal is happy, satisfied;
> but I, when lying down to rest, I am by tedium
>   assailed? . . .
>
> Or perhaps, now wanders from the truth,
> while gazing on another's fate, my thought . . .?[1]

Starting from somewhat conventional assertions, the poet's thought is gradually uplifted and, breaking its bounds, tries to penetrate into the mystery enveloping the whole of the universe. And a vague suspicion begins to form in his mind. Is even the flock of sheep, so calm and still, and apparently so contented with its lot, really entirely free from this indefinable anguish?

A cosmic anguish, this, which has also so much part in the 'sorrow' of the poet Pascoli, whose animals seem to

[1] *'Canto notturno'*, sts. v and vi. *Op. cit.*

share in it more explicitly. For instance in 'Passeri a sera',[1] he writes:

'Already the little ones sleep. Only
the old keep watch. From one comes a sigh.
Alas! at times thou[2] hast pity for us.
Just art thou, but stern in anger . . .

Now that the little ones have their heads hidden
beneath their wings, close to their hearts,
now I can say, while are silent the bees,
the flies, spiders, each thing: we must die! . . .

Oh the cruel net with which us all alive
thou snarest, great, small, so many, too many!
Oh the lightning[3] which reaches us
right on the highest tops of the poplars! . . .

But from thee comes too what pleases us:
perhaps this[4] too will bring pleasure?[5]

An innocent, trusting resignation to fate? But the anxiety which makes the little hearts beat fast has not passed away.

All this is not simply a poet's imagination. We cannot know how deep down in an animal's soul the knowledge of death may have an effect; but we can see quite clearly that animals are conscious of death. How often one sees their eyes open wide in fear; and how their little hearts can beat as if they were going to break into pieces! And when, worn out, they 'feel' that they are going to die, what passes through those tiny minds in their meek and gentle anguish?

Some problems have not yet been considered by philosophers; but poets feel the mystery of destiny weighing upon all living creatures, and they are conscious of the

---

[1] 'Passeri a sera' (Sparrows at evening), from *Canti di Castel vecchio* by Giovanni Pascoli (1855–1912).

[2] i.e., man. The bird is imagined as addressing mankind.

[3] i.e., gun-shot.

[4] i.e., death.

[5] 'Passeri a sera,' sts. vi and vii.

unasked questions which concern what is far beyond our finite existence, beyond the precise and narrow limits of what is merely of this earth. For all creatures, all souls, great and small, are aware of that quiver as of a wing that brushes by, of that shudder denoting the fulfilment of a destiny, of that tremor of a question, scarcely whispered.

Rupert Brooke, in his poem 'Heaven', thus writes of fishes:

> 'Fish (fly-replete, in depth of June,
> Dawdling away their wat'ry noon)
> Ponder deep wisdom, dark or clear,
> Each secret fishy hope or fear.
> Fish say, they have their Stream and Pond;
> But is there anything Beyond?
> This life cannot be All, they swear,
> For how unpleasant, if it were!
> One may not doubt that, somehow, Good
> Shall come of Water and of Mud;
> And, sure, the reverent eye must see
> A Purpose in Liquidity.
> We darkly know, by Faith we cry,
> The future is not Wholly Dry.
> Mud unto Mud! Death eddies near—
> Not here the appointed End, not here!
> But somewhere, beyond Space and Time,
> In wetter water, slimier slime!
> And there (they trust) there swimmeth One
> Who swam ere rivers were begun,
> Immense, of fishy form and mind,
> Squamous, omnipotent and kind;
> And under that Almighty Fin,
> The littlest fish may enter in.'[1]

One cannot deny that these dear little fishes have a somewhat unilateral conception of the world and of heaven. And perhaps we should have difficulty in recognizing our God in

[1] Rupert Brooke, 'Heaven,' 6. 1–25.

the one whose image they have formed in their minds. Yet not even St. Thomas could convict them of theological inaccuracy. For there is truly in God the cause and origin of all perfection, everything that the little fishes see in Him: even the supreme blessedness of the transcendent 'liquidity'.

Among the great lyric poets, Shelley and Keats are two who have felt most keenly the deeply spiritual quality of the song of birds, which is a voice of the soul surpassing everything that is terrestrial.

Writes Keats:

> 'Now more than ever seems it rich to die,
>   To cease upon the midnight with no pain,
>   While thou art pouring forth thy soul abroad
>   In such an ecstasy!
>   Still wouldst thou sing, and I have ears in vain—
>   To thy high requiem become a sod.
>   Thou wast not born for death, immortal Bird . . .'[1]

And Shelley in his ode 'To a Skylark':

> 'Higher still and higher
>   From the earth thou springest;
> Like a cloud of fire,
>   The deep blue thou wingest,
> And singing still dost soar and soaring ever singest.
>
> In the golden light'ning
>   Of the sunken sun,
> O'er which clouds are bright'ning,
>   Thou dost float and run,
> Like an unbodied joy whose race is just begun . . .
>
> Teach me half the gladness
>   That thy brain must know;
> Such harmonious madness
>   From my lips would flow,
> The world would listen then, as I am listening now.'[2]

[1] Keats, 'Ode to a Nightingale' sts. 6–7.
[2] Shelley, 'To a Skylark,' sts. 2–3, 21.

What can the birds' song be, or the cricket's chirruping, if not the outpouring of a soul, an outpouring of something that remains beyond our reach? Wolves howl at the moon. Bears and elephants dance, when quite alone in the secret places of their lairs. And those who have had the good fortune to see these dances say that there is something solemn and awe-inspiring about them that enthrals. What can all this mean? What does it represent?

CHAPTER NINE

The Problem of Evil

1. *In metaphysics*

IT must be recognized that it is not only in the life of man that evil is to be found. The whole of the physical universe, or at least the earth as we know it, bears evidence of deep scars left by grief.

Consider the life of a forest with its great variety of creatures. It seems, at first glance, to be something to be marvelled at and admired. But a close study of the life of its inhabitants, great and small, reveals what countless hidden dangers, what terror it contains!

It has been said that joy is more profound, more universal, than sorrow. And there is always enough joy to justify our wish to continue to live. But the suffering of an innocent creature, whether it be Abel or a tiny caterpillar, cries aloud on the whole universe for vengeance.

It is the silent reproach, which continually comes up afresh and which theology has not succeeded in stifling.

*　　　*　　　*

From a study of our world and how it is made up, the more we investigate and understand it, the more clearly we see that it all points to one supreme Intelligence; but it is not so clear that there is one supreme Goodness.

Even the reprehensible aspects of our world are counterbalanced in such careful equilibrium that we cannot help feeling immense admiration—if slightly tinged with bitterness—

for that Intelligence which orders and rules over all things.

The same could be said about the world from the aesthetic point of view. He who conceived creation is a supreme artist, and not only because of the 'idyllic' aspect of nature, if we may so call it. For tragedy, too, confers a beauty, the beauty of the majestic and the solemn, to the scene of this world.

According to theology, belief in divine goodness is maintained by saying that God 'permits' evil, not that he has intentionally created an order of this kind. This may be so. But as a 'justification' it is a poor argument. For he who permits evil to be done, when he is not so compelled, is, to a certain extent, responsible for it. Let us at least have the courage of truth, and let us not debase our idea of God.

The efforts of certain honest theologians in demonstrating that what is repugnant to us in the laws of nature is, on the contrary, 'good' or 'useful' under certain aspects, and even an element in the harmony of the universe, are very touching. Certainly, in the long run, this is so; but not in the sense in which they understand it.

Indeed, of such is the deep wisdom of God that one may say to Him: 'I do not approve of what You have done; never will I give my consent to it,' just because we are in agreement with Him. God Himself does not *approve*, and theologians may save themselves the trouble of trying to find a justification which is not required.

This problem of evil, and I am speaking here of cosmic evil (which is after all not so different from the evil properly called moral—the only difference being on whom responsibility falls), this problem should be stated as follows: It is an evil thing when a man commits a cruel deed against his brother. Can a law then be good which allows an insect to cause one of its own species to fall into a horrible trap, so that it can feed on it, by sucking its blood, while its victim is still throbbing with life?

We do not judge this law, simply because it is outside our own sphere of action. Whom can we blame for it? Nature? So thinks Leopardi, and logical coherence leads him to the negation of God: that is, God, the Highest Good, who, it is said, has created a perverse and cruel nature:

> '... to these slopes
> let him come who is wont to exalt with praise
> our human state, and let him see how much
> our race is cared for
> by a loving nature.'[1]

(If only sociologists would meditate on these lines! Leopardi shows them the road to truth. He says, in sum: before thinking out so many theories to appease discontent and class hatreds, let us recognize where the true responsibility lies: with nature. Nature, who with her laws makes of man a being ill-at-ease in this world: for he is endowed with aspirations and unlimited desires to satisfy his nobility of spirit, and at the same time he is compelled to submit to the hard necessities of material life. Society will always be more or less divided, because man bears the division within himself, and nature is hostile to him. Once having recognized this truth men will find the way to love, not by accusing one another, but by drawing close to one another for mutual defence.)

In theory at least I prefer the coherence of Leopardi to the efforts, full of praiseworthy intentions, of those who try to make appear good and necessary what is absolutely cruel, and anything but necessary for God the Omnipotent. Yet these attempts do not derive from any lack of sensibility, but from the difficulty of reconciling two truths so opposed to each other. How can one possibly say that God, the good, has created a wicked law? Since God is absolute goodness, let us say then that the law is not wicked. But, in so doing, one strikes right at the heart of divine goodness itself, which

[1] 'La Ginestra' (The Broom) from I Canti by G. Leopardi, vv. 37–41.

is the fundamental source of our capacity to judge. On the other hand, if we condemn the law, we come up against a much less difficult problem.

However sure an idea we may have of what goodness is, we shall never be able to reach the unfathomable goodness of God, which embraces the totality of being, even the farthest limits of possible things to come. And evil in itself has profound metaphysical significance: a value which (bearing in mind the 'nothingness' of Heidegger) our reason grasps and has pleasure in so doing, while our will can never consent to be the cause of evil.

If evil were simply 'lack of being' it would not have its own decisive nature, its own features. Pure negativity is formless, whereas suffering, well known to all, shows the terrible reality, the consuming power (a power which also purifies and moulds) of the thing which our conscience rejects as 'evil'. Pure negativity is inert; we cannot conceive of its being endowed with such power.

The nature of evil is a strange one. It cannot have been desired in as much as it is contrary to God (and our reason refutes it);[1] and yet it is of enormous import on the most real plane of existence; therefore, in a certain sense, it is a part of good.

We will conclude therefore that absolute evil does not exist. Evil, in an absolute sense, has no autonomy of its own. And here it is that we meet the theologians. Only (perhaps because the magnitude of the problem alarms them) they deny that evil has any metaphysical consistency. Evil does exist, however, but not separate from good. It is like

---

[1] I do not wish to confuse moral wrong, which can never be 'willed', with suffering. But let us not forget that suffering must not be willed for others, without a very good and sufficient reason, otherwise divine law is violated and we fall into sin. And to desire suffering for oneself, without a justifiable aim, seems to me to smack of the morbid and to be not far from sin, also.

Jesus's revulsion in facing the ordeal of the Passion did not derive from a simple moment of weakness of the flesh. It was something much more, a horror of the mind.

mistletoe that cannot take root without the life of a sturdy plant to support it.

The law of opposites, as well as explaining a large part of our possibility of knowledge, also contributes to the assertion of aesthetic values. Thus, suffering, in whatever way it is manifested, is translated into a value—even if not always realized by man—of art and of poetry. The most wretched aspects of nature and of life, the most mean and paltry, just because we refuse to accept them in the light of an ideal which is their opposite, acquire a poetic and dramatic quality of their own.

Are the laws of the beautiful then contrary to the needs of the heart? Is this world of ours even more monstrous in that it is actually made beautiful through our wounds and through our sorrow?

Aesthetic reality may seem inhuman, in a certain sense, in so far as it is superhuman (and because of this it belongs to that sphere of being which is part of our most innermost soul), that is, the spiritual.

The spirit has within itself such an unquenchable source of life and joy that even in experiencing sorrow, while it magnifies it (just because, by the spirit, sorrow is experienced much more profoundly than by common sensibility restricted to the life of the senses), it also takes delight in it: for this experiencing is at one and the same time knowledge and aesthetic appraisal, from which a certain measure of consent cannot be separated.

It is this, finally, that gives us the strength to exist and which justifies the world, at least in its essentials. Divine goodness, which is claimed by all the principal religions, cannot be content with righting in another world the wrongs inflicted in this. It must place 'in this world' a possibility of justification: and this is the whole life of the spirit, which is the outlet for every grief.

The actuation of this first reality is to be found in the meaning of the Redemption, with its affirmation of the redeeming value of sorrow. *But the Cross in itself is not a sufficient metaphysical justification.* God the Redeemer is the Absolute God in whom the problems of existence are clarified, before the expectancy and the promise of a redemption are made manifest.

2. *Satan and Death*

If this—from a philosophical point of view—is what counts for most, then the Revelation would allow us to go further into the question of the responsibility of created things.

Let us open the Book of Job.

God allows Satan to strike Job with every imaginable sort of evil: a thunderbolt falls from heaven, sudden wind blows down his house, a malignant ulcer corrupts his body. This story, while it reveals Satan's actual mastery over the elements, also appears as the symbol of a power conferred on him since the beginning of the world.

Let us try to imagine the angel of darkness after his rebellion, now become an enemy of God. But God does not annihilate this rebel angel, nor take from him all his intelligence and his power.

How will this boundless thirst for power be manifest, this turbulent might, which is like a cosmic force? Man has not yet appeared on the earth. It is on the elements that Satan will make his action felt, it is against them that he will loosen all his fury. And at the first appearance of life he will want to destroy it, thus becoming the lord of death.

In the gospels Satan is almost constantly called 'the prince of this world'. Such a title seems to confirm his authority not only over degenerate human nature but over nature in general.

If we examine a declaration which is particularly significant: 'Hereafter I will not talk much with you, for the prince of this world cometh,'[1] it seems as if death is identical with the person of Satan.

It will be objected: 'What is said here alludes to the powers of darkness gaining the ascendency with the condemnation and the crucifixion of the Son of God.' In substance it is of this that Jesus wishes to speak. But let us not deprive words of their true weight. The 'prince of this world' is the same one who unleashed against Job all the fury of the elements and who tortured him with illness, the same to whom Christ ascribes his own death.

'For God created man to be immortal, and made him to an image of his own eternity. Nevertheless through envy of the devil came death into the world: and they that do hold of his side do find it.'[2]

The cause of death is sin, says St. Paul; that is, of universal death, not only of the death of mankind. But animals had not committed any sin to make them responsible for their own death.

Theology speaks of 'preternatural exemption' from suffering and from death; while they (suffering and death) are, essentially, *against nature*, even if they already existed *in fact*, having been introduced by a mysterious power. I am speaking, of course, of true death, of the final end of all things, not of the inevitable passing from this life.

If transitoriness is the law of this world, if living beings have a limited period for their earthly existence, let it not be calmly said that physical death, as it is, is natural; natural and necessary the terrifying destruction of the elements. For then death seems more like murder than a passing on.

---

[1] John XIV, 30-1.
[2] Wisdom of Solomon II, 23-5.

3. *Eve's choice*

The moment has come for us to face the problem of original sin. Whatever may have actually happened (commentators do not agree on the interpretation of the Bible, which may have a more or less literal meaning, and a mystical or imaginatively intuitive sense), it is certain that the biblical story in its spontaneity and directness sums up in a few vivid touches a tragedy that humanity has always felt deep down; a tragedy which has found corresponding expression in remote traditions of almost all the ancient peoples.

This 'remote tradition' consoles man, by inducing him to believe in the absolute goodness of God and in the existence of a primitive world (in both a chronological and an ideal sense) more perfect than our own.

The revolt of Adam and Eve, or rather, their choice (the biblical images, whether corresponding exactly or not to something that really happened, are highly expressive) is, in part, at the root of all the misfortune of humanity; and it makes its effects felt on creatures nearest to us.

And yet, would we dare to condemn our ancestors? It would have been cowardly to draw back when on the very threshold of the mystery: 'If you eat of that fruit, you will have knowledge of good and of evil.'

Is it the mark of a strong spirit to resist the temptation of wanting to know? Eve gave way, in spite of her fear of divine anger. And God—I have no hesitation in saying—expected this revolt, which was the first action involving risk, the first assertion of the personality of 'nascent' humanity. Eve took the risk, bringing down on her its consequences. Her gesture inspires reverence.

But Eve soon drew back. If she is to blame, it is for not daring to face the Almighty with the calm glance of a conscious spirit. Weakness and fear took the upper hand. 'And they hid themselves.'

If only they had said: "You could not ask us *not to want to know*!" Here was the test, and this was the reply that would have saved them.

But let us not expect more of them. Their mad audacity is the light which illumines humanity from its beginnings. It was too early then for the consciousness which humanity was to acquire in its long journey. What God did not have from them, He is waiting to receive, in the course of the millennia, from their descendants.

Thought does not fear God, and God does not reprove revolt suggested by thought. He does not want servants or slaves, and not even children who are too obedient. He wants us to speak to Him, as one spirit to another. Only then will He be satisfied, for He will then see that He has truly created man.

4. *Animals and sorrow*

But let us return to the animals.

> Peace, this universe of ours can never have,
>   while there is still a tremor
> of the echo of that cry.[1]

They suffer and we do not know why. As a reflection of man's suffering, or of the perverse power of Satan, or because of the approval of God, who does not wish to leave them out of the titanic drama of created things?

But all suffering claims a catharsis. It cannot be an end in itself, it must be transferred on to another plane. Otherwise, when even a little sparrow or a kitten dies, our horror would have no end.

[1] The author's own verses.

CHAPTER TEN

Animals and Holy Scripture

1. *Animals and the Old Testament*

'I SAID in my heart concerning the state of the sons of men:
God shows them that they might see that they themselves
are like beasts. For that which befalleth the sons of men
befalleth beasts; even one thing befalleth them. As the one
dieth, so dieth the other; yea, they have all one breath; so
that a man hath no pre-eminence above a beast: for all is
vanity. All go into one place; all are of the dust, and all turn
to dust again. Who knoweth that the spirit of man goeth
upward, and that the spirit of the beast goeth downward
under the earth?'[1]

From this it will be seen that in the times of Ecclesiastes
man had already acquired the habit of comparing himself
with animals so as to feel his superiority over them; while
the critically impartial attitude of the writer of these verses
is, indeed, rather different from the general one. From the
relatively pessimistic character of the book it is evident that
the author's intention is not to exalt the animal world, but
rather to make a melancholy comparison between animals
and man.

The question asked, however, is about the destination of
souls, not about their survival, which here seems to be
accepted beyond all doubt. In fact Ricciotti makes the
following comment: 'The problem that the author considers

---

[1] Ecclesiastes III, 18–21, Authorized Version, with slight variations. Quotations
from the Bible are given in the Authorized Version, with, when necessary, slight
variations so as to conform closely to the Italian, taken from the Vulgate.

here is, from all appearances, of a topographical nature. He is convinced that the human "soul" after death goes down into Sceol, or the lower regions (see vv.9 and 10) and that it returns to God (see vv. 12 and 7); but here he seems to be asking himself whether the "breath" or source of physiological life of the beast goes into a different place from man's "breath", seeing that physiological death is precisely the same in both (see v. 19), where the term "breath"—the Hebrew *ruah*—is used as here. Some think that this is a rhetorical question, challenging science, natural science and physiology, to offer an answer to this difficult problem.'[1]

Quite apart from the specific linguistic problem, it is clear from the context that the word 'breath' has a much wider meaning here than that of simply the 'source of physiological life', and that it is much nearer to our own term 'spirit'. But Ricciotti is not concerned with the examination of this problem.

The implications of the last two verses are very significant. If taken in isolation, they assume a playfully malicious tone, quite contrary to the general attitude of the book. We may develop the substance of their meaning as follows: who can say whether, in the next life, many men who now think themselves so superior will not be judged extremely severely, while the souls of some of the innocent animals may find themselves in a much more fortunate position?

Let us answer the following question truthfully, and without false pride: is the soul of a selfish miser, full of deceit and meanness, really nearer to God than that of a pretty little fawn, or of a poor baby rabbit, or of a mother cat who lovingly suckles her little ones? The writer of the Book of Wisdom is very far-seeing. Beyond all question man's soul is a step higher in the hierarchy than the souls of animals. But . . . it is all the same very difficult to make certain

[1] G. Ricciotti, *Note a la Sacra Bibbia*, ed. Salani.

I

comparisons. Who can ever know which will be judged the more valuable in the presence of the majesty of God?

The story of Balaam and the ass seems central to this group of ideas:

'And Balaam rose up in the morning, and saddled his ass, and went with them [the princes of Moab]. And God's anger was kindled because he went; and the angel of the Lord stood in the way as an adversary against him. Now he was riding upon his ass, and two servants were with him. And the ass saw the angel of the Lord standing in the way, and his sword drawn in his hand: and the ass turned aside and went into the fields: and Balaam smote the ass, to turn her into the way. But the angel of the Lord stood in a path of the vineyards, a wall being on this side and a wall on that side. And when the ass saw the angel of the Lord, she thrust herself into the wall, and crushed Balaam's foot against the wall: and he smote her again. And the angel of the Lord went further, and stood in a narrow place, where was no way to turn either to the right hand or to the left. And when the ass saw the angel of the Lord, she fell down under Balaam: and Balaam's anger was kindled, and he smote the ass with a staff. And the Lord opened the mouth of the ass; and she said unto Balaam: What have I done unto thee, that thou has smitten me these three times? And Balaam said unto the ass: Because thou hast mocked me: I would there were a sword in mine hand, for now I would kill thee. And the ass said unto Balaam: Am I not thine ass, upon which thou has ridden ever since I was thine unto this day? Was I ever wont to do such things unto thee? And he replied: Never. Then the Lord opened the eyes of Balaam, and he saw the angel of the Lord standing in the way, with his sword drawn in his hand; and he bowed down his head and fell flat on his face. And the angel of the Lord said unto him: Wherefore hast thou smitten thine ass these three times? Behold I went out to withstand thee, because thy way is perverse before me; and the ass saw me, and turned from me these three times; unless she had turned from me, surely now also I had slain thee, and saved her alive.'[1]

This is the amazing Bible story, and from it we may make two important observations: first, the angel reprimands Balaam for having beaten his ass; the reproof here is quite indisputable and shows clearly that it is a mistake to think that man will not be called to give account to God for the way in which he treats animals. Secondly there is a comparison between the behaviour of the ass and the behaviour of Balaam, entirely to the advantage of the former (even though Balaam was a prophet). There is a benevolent attitude towards the ass, who in any case would have been spared; while Balaam himself would have been killed, if his beast had not saved him.

It is not so very extraordinary that the ass should notice the angel before its master did. It has been known since early times that animals are more susceptible than man to the supernatural, and this has been confirmed by recent studies in psychical research.[2] But it is extraordinary that the ass should begin to speak. This fact, however, does not relegate the Balaam episode to a class of events having no meaning for our ordinary everyday life.

We must determine what is meant by a miracle. When a miracle happens, it is something outside the laws of contingent reality—and therefore we could imagine worlds where this reality is completely different—*but a miracle is never contrary to the superior laws of reason.*

Or it may be stated thus: it is quite abnormal for the ass to speak; but what it says is perfectly logical. It is abnormal for a very sick man to be cured suddenly; but such an

[1] Numbers XXII, 21–33 (A.V., slightly altered).
[2] Cf. *Op. cit.* Ernesto Bozzano, *Gli Animali Hanno un' Anima?*

occurrence is within reason, because of the mercy of God and as a demonstration of his mastery over the laws of nature. Indeed, it is the abnormal aspect in a miracle which serves to bring into evidence superior spiritual truths, for the abnormality presents them so much more strikingly.

In this connection, particularly significant is the historic miracle which happened at Turin in 1453, the so-called miracle of the Sacrament, in which an ass kneels down to worship the Blessed Sacrament, hidden in a sack with valuables which thieves had stolen from a church in Exilles.

This miraculous incident, as well as serving to show the divine and inviolable nature of the Eucharist—which called forth an act of worship on the part of an ass—seems also to make use of the last mentioned to make it quite clear that homage is due to God from all His creatures. In fact it would appear that here the contrast is purposely brought out: that is, in comparison with, and in reproof of, the evil conduct of men, we are given the example of the good behaviour of an animal. (I myself firmly believe that animals have a relationship with God; and not one of dependence only, but of a more intimate kind. Some sort of inner relationship must exist, suited to the simple, spontaneous, non-meditative nature of their souls.)

The meek and much-scorned little donkey (the wild ass of the Scriptures) seems to have a special place of honour in the sight of God. In addition to the praises of the angel in the Balaam story, to the poetical description in the book of Job, and to the important part played by the donkey in the miracle of the Sacrament just quoted, it is the ass that will be chosen to carry the Saviour in triumph to Jerusalem. And with what gentle kindness Our Lord treated it we shall see later in the Gospel according to St. Matthew.

To bring to an end our evidence from the Old Testament, I cannot afford to neglect one of the stories which gives most vivid expression to this biblical attitude of sensitiveness to animals:

'And the Lord sent Nathan unto David. And he came unto him and said unto him: "There were two men in one city; one rich and the other poor. The rich man had exceeding many flocks and herds; but the poor man had nothing save one little ewe lamb, which he had bought and nourished up; and it grew up together with him and his children; it did eat of his own bread, and drank of his own cup, and lay in his bosom, and was unto him as a daughter. And there came a traveller unto the rich man; and he, wishing to spare his own flock and his own herd, to prepare a banquet for the wayfarer that was come unto him, took the poor man's lamb, and dressed it for the man that had come unto him. And David's anger was greatly kindled against the man; and he said to Nathan, "As the Lord liveth! the man that has done this thing is deserving of death; and he shall restore the lamb fourfold, for having committed this crime and for not having spared the sheep." But Nathan said to David: "Thou art that man!" ' [1]

The allusion to the wife of Uriah is well known. Without realizing the comparison with himself, David is not surprised at the behaviour of the poor man, who loves his sheep and treats it 'as a daughter'; he even proclaims the man who took it from him guilty of punishment by death. And it should be noted that he would have compelled him 'to restore the lamb fourfold' not only for the material loss sustained, but because he had not 'spared the sheep'; the sheep considered not just as an object, but almost as a person. Such is the meaning of the comparison made by the prophet; if it were not so, the parallel would not hold.

The Old Testament, therefore, at times so implacable in comparison with the New Law, has nevertheless words

[1] II Samuel XII, 1-7, (A.V., slightly altered).

expressing great benevolence and gentleness towards animals.

But we may go further. That animals have a certain kind of ethical personality may be deduced from some expressions which would seem inconceivable if this order of ideas was not accepted.

Let us recall the Covenant with Noah:

'. . . And surely your blood of your lives will I require; at the hand of every beast will I require it . . . Whoso sheddeth man's blood, by man shall his blood be shed; for in the image of God made he man.'[1]

This passage will permit one to presume that deep down in their inmost being, from a primeval instinct from remote ages, animals 'know' that they should not kill man.

One could say, in fact, that before God they have what we might term (so as to render the idea) a legal personality. This is also confirmed by the fact that the Covenant is made with them too:

'And God spake unto Noah and to his sons with him, saying: And behold I establish my covenant with you and with your seed after you; and with every living creature that is with you, of the fowl, of the cattle, and of every beast of the earth with you; from all that go out of the ark, to every beast of the earth. And I will establish my covenant with you; neither shall all flesh be cut off any more by the waters of a flood; neither shall there be any more a flood to destroy the earth. And God said: This is the token of the covenant which I make between me and you and every living creature that is with you, for all future generations: I will place my rainbow in the clouds, and it shall be a token between me and the earth. When I have covered the heaven with clouds, my bow shall appear in the clouds; and I will remember my covenant, which is between me and you and every living creature of all flesh; and the waters shall no more become a

[1] Genesis IX, 5–6.

flood to destroy all living creatures. And my bow shall be in the clouds; and I shall look upon it, that I may remember the everlasting covenant between God and every living creature of all flesh that is upon the earth.[1]

2. *Animals and the Gospels*

Gospel sayings regarding animals are, I would say, less patriarchal and more lyrical in tone than in the Old Testament, less solemn and more emotional in appeal.

The Son of God uses words of great tenderness when speaking of these, his smaller creatures:

'O Jerusalem, Jerusalem, thou that killest the prophets, and stonest them that are sent unto thee, how often would I have gathered thy children together, even as a hen gathereth her chickens under her wings, and ye would not!'[2]

'If a man have a hundred sheep, and one of them be gone astray, doth he not leave the ninety and nine, and goeth into the mountains, and seeketh that which has gone astray? And if so be that he find it, verily I say unto you, he rejoiceth more of that sheep, than of the ninety and nine which went not astray.'[3]

We have already had occasion to note that the images and parables of the Gospels are much less symbolical than representative. They do not deal with references in the abstract, but with concrete representations which are so sensitive and alive that one feels that they are of importance to the Divine Master in themselves, almost as much as the meaning underlying them. Is more tenderness felt for the sinner, or for the sheep that was lost? On the plane of emotion and of poetry, it is difficult to find an answer.

[1] Genesis IX, 8–16 (A.V., slightly altered).
[2] Matthew XXIII, 37 Luke XIII, 34 (A.V., slightly altered).
[3] Matthew XVIII, 19 (A.V., slightly altered).

'But he that entereth in by the door is the shepherd of the sheep. To him the porter openeth; and the sheep hear his voice . . . But a stranger they will not follow, but will flee from him; for they know not the voice of strangers.'[1]

It is true that there are other passages in which animals are mentioned where the aim is to give prominence to their inferiority:

'Let the children first be fed; for it is not meet to take the children's bread and cast it to the dogs.' But the Canaanite mother (the woman of Canaan) promptly replied: 'True Lord, yet the dogs eat of the crumbs which fall from their master's table.'[2]

And the Lord immediately approves what she says.

All this is very far removed from the rhetorical. The Divine Master's smiles and parables are so closely connected to life that one cannot doubt the exactness with which He sees qualities and sentiments taking shape in animals, qualities and sentiments which we call 'human', as if they belonged exclusively to us. He 'sees' the mother-love of the hen, the innocence of the dove, the wisdom of the serpent; for Him the incommensurable abyss placed by man between men and animals does not exist. His comparisons have the spontaneity and certainty of one who recognises a real correspondence between the two terms; or—on different planes—the same world of values applicable to each.

And lastly, there is a most subtle lesson taught, not by words, but by example. The Gospel stories relate how Jesus made his triumphal entry into Jerusalem riding on an ass. But St. Matthew alone adds this detail:

'And when they drew nigh unto Jerusalem, and were come to Bethphage, near the Mount of Olives, then sent Jesus two disciples, saying unto them: 'Go into the village over against

[1] John X, 2–5.
[2] Matthew XV, 26–7.

you, and straightway ye shall find an ass tied, and a colt with her: loose them and bring them unto me.'[1]

Jesus only had need of one, the colt; but quite clearly he did not want to take it away from its mother and leave her in anxiety about it. And in the triumphal procession the ass walks by the side of her colt. Why has no one pointed out the lesson this implies?

In the church of St. Germain des Prés, in Paris, there is a wonderfully expressive fresco, depicting this scene, which only differs from the text of the Gospels in one particular: Jesus is riding on the ass and the colt is following just behind.[2]

Some practical-minded people may say that the ass might have been of use as well. But they were already in sight of Jerusalem, there was not very much more distance to go. However that may be, one cannot help noting the tender care shown towards the animal mother and her son. It is most fortunate that St. Matthew has not left out this human touch, which, apparently insignificant, is yet of so great value.

*   *   *

The neglect of the relationship between God and the animal world, with the consequent setting of man as the absolute centre, is a serious omission in biblical exegesis. For this unilateral vision makes the Holy Scripture less forceful and narrows its scope, by thus dimming the radiance of its poetical and dramatic qualities.

But, we may ask: why do the Holy Scriptures not reach more explicit declarations with regard to our problem?

If everything has not been clearly revealed, this is so as not

---

[1] Matthew XXI, 1–2 (A.V., slightly altered).
[2] Translator's note: This second version is the one followed in the English A.V.

to stifle that spirit in man which thirsts for knowledge; and in this connection it is wonderful to see how God, while enlightening us sufficiently, yet leaves it to our charity to draw the final conclusions.

We must not ask Him to tell us. It is up to us ourselves to rise above our paltry attitude of self-interest and to realize what our duty is to these small companions of our earthly existence. It is strange that it seems to cost us so much to do so.

It is true that we have neither the possibility nor the right to take from them what is their own true nature. But such realization—which does not in any way change reality—is indeed an act of justice and of comprehension, which it is our duty to perform.

CHAPTER ELEVEN

Is it Right to Kill Animals?

1. *A primordial sacrifice*

LET us not leave the sphere of Holy Scripture before examining another problem, which in theory should not be of vital importance to the aims of our argument, but which is so, in the opinion of many.

Why, these people ask, may we kill animals in order to eat them without breaking any moral law? And they conclude: clearly because animals have no soul.

But this is to infer something quite arbitrarily. In special cases, as, for example, in lawful defence, it is permitted to kill a man, and that does not in any way compromise the immortality of his soul. And further: if suicide is unlawful, it is nevertheless praiseworthy and heroic to sacrifice one's life for one's fellow creatures, or for an ideal. Suicide, no; that is not lawful; but sacrifice, immolation, yes.

The case of the animals is analogous. To provide us with food, they are not being killed because they have no natural right to live; in reality they are being sacrificed with the object of preserving the life of superior beings.

And when animals eat each other? This is the same cruel and inevitable law of nature which is being enforced.

They are all lives *sacrificed*. And this fact not only does not prejudge the value of the souls of the victims; on the contrary it claims for them, with a far better right, that justice will later be done them.

Could we stop eating animals? I do not want to be a propagandist for vegetarian theories here; that would take me right away from the intention of this study. Perhaps we could, but, in the condition of things as they are at the present, it might be harmful to our development and to our vitality.

However, I should like to quote biblical evidence. After having created man and woman, God said to them:

'Behold, I have given you every herb bearing seed, which is upon the face of all the earth, and every tree, in the which is the fruit of a tree yielding seed; *to you it shall be for meat*; and to every beast of the earth, and to every fowl of the air, and to every thing that creepeth on the earth, wherein there is life, I have given every green herb for meat . . .'[1]

Further on this idea is confirmed. Thus God turns to Adam and says:

'. . . cursed is the ground because of what thou hast done; in sorrow shalt thou eat of it all the days of thy life; thorns also and thistles shall it bring forth to thee; and *thou shalt eat the herb of the field*.'[2]

Therefore we must note that, according to the original order of creation, products of the vegetable kingdom, and only these, were to be used for food for all living creatures.

Only later, after the Flood, in the solemn Covenant, was permission given for man to feed on animals.

'God blessed Noah and his sons, and said unto them: "Be fruitful and multiply, and replenish the earth. And the fear of you and the dread of you shall be upon every beast of the earth, and upon every fowl of the air, upon all that moveth upon the earth, and upon all the fishes of the sea; into your hand are they entrusted. Every moving thing that liveth shall be meat for you; even as the green herb, have I given you all things. But flesh with the life thereof, which is the blood thereof, shall ye not eat. And surely your blood of your lives will I require; at the hand of every beast will I

---

[1] Genesis I, 29–30 (A.V., slightly altered).
[2] Genesis III, 17–18.

require it, and at the hand of man; at the hand of every man's brother will I require the life of man.'[1]

But this came later, to set things right again after the rebellion, when disobedience and crime already reigned supreme on earth.

We cannot go into questions of chronology. When, and in what geological era, did animals begin to devour each other? The dinosaurs and other monsters who inhabited the earth before the Flood appear to have been vegetarians. At any rate it seems to me that the events related in Genesis are only apparently chronological, and should be understood as having an ideal sequence.

Holy Scripture informs us that, according to the original ideal order of creation, this killing of each other among living creatures ought never to have happened. All this confirms my belief set out above that not all the laws of nature have originated directly from God. Not all of them, in fact, reflect clearly the spirit of supreme good.

Meditation on this problem leads to some considerations of an ethical order. Animals were 'entrusted' to man, not given into his absolute power. We may make use of them wisely and mercifully and we shall have to give account to God for the way in which we have used our authority over them.

Therefore it is (perhaps) permissible to kill them; but only when it is necessary, and we must make them suffer as little as possible, under penalty of sinning against natural law. The same may be said with regard to the use of animals for scientific experiments.

In conclusion, if animals are sacrificed on our account, we must acknowledge this sacrifice; and we must treat with respect these beings which nature compels us to make our victims. Indeed, some little gratitude would not be out of place.

One last consideration. Extremely horrible is the custom of killing animals in the most cruel way so that the food

[1] Genesis IX, 1–5.

produced is more tasty, as sometimes happens. Sacrifice them in order to keep us alive, if we must; but make them suffer more so as to enhance the pleasures of our palate, this we must not do. It is a vile and a dastardly thing. Animals such as lobsters, snails, and frogs[1] ought not to be killed, if a more painless method cannot be found. If we are compelled (or so is generally believed) to make them endure so cruel a death, it is far preferable not to kill them at all, but to let them live.

2. *Animals and vivisection*

At this juncture we must approach the very painful subject of vivisection; a subject which is, in general, very little known, as these practices (of which unhappily there is not the slightest doubt) are carried out secretly in the seclusion of experimental laboratories.

To avoid misunderstandings we must at once distinguish between legitimate experiment and vivisection: to the latter we give the general and current meaning of tampering with animals so as to cause them pain beyond the limit of what can be suffered and so may be termed cruelty.

There is at present a kind of mania for vivisectional experiment, even in ordinary teaching, where there is not even the excuse of research. Instead of using photographs, drawings, models and the vast amount of excellent material that teaching now has at its disposal, we have even reached the stage of cutting open the body of live animals for the most commonplace demonstrations. (Young students, why do you not rebel against such methods?)

And to what end is all this done? The difference between

[1] According to the rule laid down by the Society for the Prevention of Cruelty to Animals, frogs ought to be beheaded straight away. But it seems that this rule is not always kept.

the animal and the human organism, just as the difference between organisms from one animal to another, not only makes this quite unjustifiable but can actually lead to serious mistakes. Eminent scientists, among whom we may mention Augusto Murri, have declared themselves in the name of science quite opposed to such methods of investigation.

Here is the opinion of Dr. Gennaro Ciaburri, whose book,[1] written objectively and with a painful lucidity, gives an idea of the crime with which humanity is defiled behind the all too obliging screen of science.

'The craze for experiment in medicine is becoming a real disease. All doctors and teachers who think and reflect on the subject agree that this is so; but few and only on rare occasions raise their voices to say: *Put a stop to it*.

'The facility with which material can be obtained, the easy way open to all those who think that, by cutting a piece of flesh in this or that part of the body, they can gather together evidence of knowledge necessary to give them *qualifications* for a University lectureship or a post in this or that institution, help to keep this method in force, although it has been condemned by some of the greatest names in Medicine.' (Chapter IV, 'Vivisection as a method of scientific investigation'.)

We as laymen would like to add, with due humility: Is this excessive use of experiment really consistent with the dignity of science? Should not intuition and deduction, that is, intelligence, in fact, be the first guide to comprehension? It is well known that scientists who are truly constructive and who make really useful discoveries do not belong to the ranks of the vivisectionists, even if on a rare occasion they are compelled to make use of such experiments legitimately.

Having stated this, there are still many reasons against the use of vivisection: reasons of a moral order, reasons

---

[1] *La sperimentazione sugli animali.*

connected with our sensibility, our compassion and, above all, with our sense of justice. The reader who has followed me so far will—I hope—be convinced that animals have a true soul, peculiar to them, capable of enjoyment and of suffering. (A very significant integral part of their psyche is a sense of *amazement* which has been noted in these victims even by the most remorseless torturers when carrying out investigations!) Therefore, if we admit that man, by reason of his superior status, is permitted to make legitimate use of animals, he is certainly not allowed to go beyond certain limits.

But what is considered a 'legitimate' use? It is very difficult to answer that question truly in this world of light and shadow, where we are compelled to accept compromise and where war is allowed. But all the same an answer must be found. So as to draw a line of demarcation between the so-called rights of science and the superior demands of ethics, I feel that the following principle must be accepted: animals may be made use of when necessary to further the cause of science (but only when *absolutely necessary*); and due precautions should always be taken, for we must remember that they are creatures with feeling and to a certain extent conscious of what is happening, and any form of cruelty should be absolutely forbidden.

The state of things with regard to vivisection is not generally known to the public, both because those who practise it are careful not to advertise the fact, and because of the comforting reason that the common man, in his honest respect for science and in his knowledge that the use of anaesthetics is now so perfected, does not doubt that everything is carried out with due care. How can doctors and scientists, who are working for the good of humanity, for the relief of pain, bring themselves to show cruelty towards animals? Is it to be believed that research workers improve their knowledge by inflicting without care or scruple unheard-of suffering on defenceless creatures? This is, quite clearly, the opinion of the ordinary person. But we cannot deceive ourselves, at least as regards certain types of experiment, which are, of necessity, cruel in themselves. Certain terrible kinds of experiment with regard to the nervous system, for instance, on reactions to burns and similar pains do not leave much room for optimism. Nor does the thought of an anaesthetic allay our anxiety in such matters as, for instance, symbiosis.

These are all very sad topics. Do they not make us feel that even the rights of science should go only to a limit set by our conscience, and that beyond that limit we may not go?

On the question of vivisection opinions are too much in disagreement. Anyone who tries to enter into the discussion finds himself in dangerous waters. To steer his way in them, in addition to superior ethical principles as his guide, he needs to have as well a very firm foundation of up-to-date and expert information of the work going on. Those who wish to protect animals intervene, but they end by finding themselves in difficulties. Working against them, on the one hand, is the lack (in theory) of a recognition of any general principle (e.g., have animals rights?); and, on the other, the inferiority complex of the layman as opposed to the professional.

* * *

In order to untie this knot, the chief aid should come from the objective, scrupulous goodwill of the scientists themselves. They, more than anyone else, must feel responsibility for this problem. I shall quote some information and declarations from the review: *Scienza e coscienza* (*Science and Conscience*),[1] the name of which quite clearly indicates the

[1] Bologna, *Scienza e Coscienza* (Official organ of the Union of Italian antivivisectionists).

poles between which move the investigations of men who are in a position to take true stock of the situation.

It is undoubtedly true that the most serious research workers have travelled along the main road of research by anatomical dissection of corpses and by clinical observation of man himself.

'The conclusions of the famous nerve-specialist Hughlings Jackson (London 1834–1911) reached by him from examination of diseased persons and corpses, and on which modern science with regard to cerebral localizations is based, were arrived at without any experiments made on animals. Illustrations of the brain published later by F. Krause and by others have not added any new contribution to what had been previously ascertained.' (Maximilian Rakette, *Scienza e Coscienza*. April–June 1959.)

And as regards the aims of the teacher: 'In a film everything can be seen far better, particularly because the image is presented greatly enlarged, and, projected on to the screen, it can then be seen by many students in the very large halls like those of our largest Universities.'

These are constructive suggestions of a scientist who keeps all the problems in mind, and who tries to find the best solution for them by making proposals which neither common sense nor the scientific spirit can refute.

In particular he deplores useless experiments, repeated indefinitely, without a thought of putting out to interest at a hundred per cent, with accurate deductions and conclusions, the painful sacrifice already made of one animal.

'Symbiosis is the joining together of two animals by means of the stitching of the abdominal parts, which have previously been cut open. The animals scream and groan dreadfully, and such a spectacle is truly terribly pitiful. Following such joining certain organs are excluded, as, for example, the kidney, the liver and sometimes even the extremities. Death generally follows six weeks or so afterwards. As far as I know there are quite a number of works already on this subject, and therefore it is quite incomprehensible why such experiments are ever repeated.'

'In the latest publications of Professor Hess, at the side of the text in German, an English version is also printed. This new departure is to be recommended as a protection for animals, so that some experiments are not repeated when it is known that they have already been performed.'

'If one attends a medical Congress, as I so often do, one hears a long series of papers in which experiments on animals are mentioned in most widely differing fields. When it becomes clear that such experiments have little reliability, it is very surprising that these researchers do not draw their own conclusions from logical argument; but instead they nearly always refer to further experiments they are to carry out. But in the numerous publications on the subject in medical reviews, one always finds that only negative or doubtful results are obtained from such experiments.

'Investigation cannot claim to give a place of authority to experimental methods. Much new knowledge can only be the result of rigorous, logical thought and deep meditation or of profound observation.' (Maximilian Rakette, art. cit.)

Vivisection is the great problem for these creatures who are destined to cross the treacherous sea of life in our company. According to the *Coalition Mondiale contre la Vivisection*, which has its headquarters at Geneva, the number of animals sacrificed each year for experiments (either with or without anaesthetic, with due precautions for their suffering or complete indifference to it) is forty million. *Forty million* defenceless living beings, virtually at the mercy of the conscience, human and Christian, of those experimenting on them!

* * *

When I spoke above about the lack of any recognition of a principle, I meant an official, legal recognition. In general the law protects animals from the cruelties of vivisection. It insists particularly on the absolute necessity for the experiment, on the use of an anaesthetic, on accurate inspection and reporting, on the prohibiting of the use of an animal for more than one experiment, if it survives the first. But the rare, exceptional cases, which are allowed, if only cautiously, by the legislators, open the door to all kinds of infringement. The laws do exist; but all too frequently they are not enforced.

On what rights are these laws founded? The original motive usually alleged for them—and it is the same that induced Pope St. Pius Vth to condemn bull-fights in 1567— is the incompatibility of the human spirit with all forms of cruelty: a definite argument (how very definite, we have seen!) from man's point of view, but still insufficient.

Although law and religion have not yet sanctioned any official recognition of the rights of animals (not even a right to be spared if their death is not absolutely necessary to man; and to be killed without cruelty if and when they are condemned to death), we must not forget that law and religion are both founded on natural law. It is the part of man's own conscience to tell him that it is not permitted, that it is unjust and morally base to behave cruelly to other creatures. If the soul of animals has not yet received a precise definition,[1] nor definite recognition, because man has not made sufficient study of it, our own sensibility, our intuition, and our innate fellowship with all creatures should help to make us feel that there is this ethical relationship.

---

[1] *Coscienza aurorali* (Auroral consciences) is the definition suggested by Mons. Vincenzo Arcozzi-Masino.

CHAPTER TWELVE

Merit and Reward: Crime and Punishment

WE now come to the consideration of a question which the reader has probably been expecting since the beginning of this book.

I think I have demonstrated sufficiently that the soul of animals is *immaterial* and belongs to the realm of the spirit; and I have clarified the concept of virtue as manifest in them. As a consequence we are faced with the idea of reward, implied in virtue, for justice demands that virtue receives its suitable reward.

But it may be said that against the idea of merit and reward must be set the opposites: wrong-doing and punishment. Can animals really sin? Are they deserving of punishment?

In general I would reply with an axiom which at first seems absurd: and that is, that *animals are capable of goodness, but not of sin; they are deserving only of reward, not of punishment.*

For the ideas of responsibility, virtue and reward lead us to consider the nature of *free will* and to ask whether animals are also in truth endowed with it. Categorical declarations, made all too hastily, fall into the risk of over-simplification; we require here at least an attempt at a definition.

I would suggest that the term *absolute free will* is not in accordance with the responsibility of animals. It involves a far wider horizon, a range over and beyond good and evil.

But animals move, function and live on this side of the limits of good. *The animal soul, both because of its simplicity, and because in it there was no original rebellion, still lives in the law of*

God. It cannot wish evil, in as much as that would be rebellion against God.

This may be taken as a general principle. However, owing to the discord in nature, animals too may have aggressive tendencies, even downright wicked ones; and they are capable of actions which border on crime.

I have already mentioned the vindictiveness of some wild beasts in captivity, who are capable of nursing their revenge for several years. And I myself had occasion to witness what was, I believe, a repeated attempt at wilful murder. This is what happened: we had a little puppy of two months old who had had to have one of his paws put into plaster of Paris. In the house there was also a cat, of a rather wild and savage nature. Quite unaccountably and in contrast to her character, we used to find her bending over the basket where little Farfui lay and licking him with a maternal tenderness. I did not trust her entirely, and so I once pretended to go out of the room, but instead I stayed just inside, where she could not see me, to watch what would happen. The moment she thought I had gone, the cat seized the puppy by its throat. I went in quickly, other members of the family came in too and the cat then reverted to her motherly behaviour. But again, a second time, as soon as she was alone she jumped on to the puppy and made as if to strangle it. Naturally we gave up any further tests, and the would-be assassin was sent away to a place less favourable for her exploits.

What shall we say about this? It is not possible to deny the actual facts. To get our bearings I will quote the rigid, classical, catholic distinction between mortal sin and venial sin. The first—in committing which there comes into action that conscious awareness, that ranging between good and evil which we call *free will*—is a wilful rebellion against God (in as much as He is God), and it is therefore irreparable unless it is consciously renounced. (This, so far as theory goes. In fact, from a psychological point of view, I am not sure at what stage one may say that the requirements for full conscious awareness are to be found in man; for this awareness presupposes a whole world of thought and experience.) Venial sin, on the other hand, is essentially a giving way to bad tendencies, to instincts, which are removed from the divine law.

An example will show immediately how—having allowed for the due difference between man and animal—in this latter sphere certain sins are found possible among animals; and how animals too can at times go against their instincts.

I once had a cat who was subject to sudden terrible outbursts of temper. It would scream like a mad thing, raise its paws to scratch, but then draw in its claws. When it got to the very height of its fit of rage, it would suddenly go off and mutter in a corner, evidently so as not to do something dreadful. As a matter of fact, if we watch our animals carefully, we shall find that almost always, after a sudden outburst of bad temper, they seem embarrassed and try in one way or another to excuse themselves. I have earlier quoted an example in an animal of what we would certainly call 'remorse'.

What shall we say about the truly 'black souls', the wilful murderers? Such calculating coolness is the result of passion, rancour, jealousy, vindictiveness, as it is among men. But all this remains implicit in animals, it has not yet reached that metaphysical responsibility, that wilful negation of the Divinity which is the sin attributed to Lucifer. Animals cannot accomplish so much. All the same, may not a kind of discriminating justice descend upon them also?

I would reply, Yes: and in clarification I would add: to a kind of venial sin there may correspond, in this life or in some other, something which we could call punishment (though it may be that the inner dissatisfaction caused by the sin itself would be penalty enough); or perhaps there may be a lessening of happiness.

Let it not be forgotten that this too is relative to the kind and to the degree of happiness to which we are called. Matching the responsibility of man's free will is man's destiny; and this is incomparably of a superior order to that of the animals.

In simple language, the less the risk, the less the recompense. (Let this be said for those who are easily alarmed and who might think that the lot of animals was a privileged one.)

CHAPTER THIRTEEN

Final Conclusions

1. The 'soul of the world'

REGARDING insects and such species as have a less individualized personality than the superior animals, and whose
intelligence—in many cases amazing—is intimately linked
with the instinct of their species, Maeterlinck[1] suggests that
after death they return to the 'collective soul'. This
suggestion is, however, 'provisional' and 'awaiting our
further knowledge'. Thus, he says, they partake of their own
special destiny of immortality or of 'an indefinite length of
time'. But 'indefinite length of time' leads one to think of a
purely terrestrial fate, while in other parts of his work this
author speaks of 'another world' and 'another plane of
life'.

Inscrutable is the mystery confronting us, particularly
concerning this undecipherable 'soul of the world'. In a
certain sense we may imagine this as a centralizing, con-
trolling, stabilizing force; taking it that God intervenes in the
life of the universe not directly, but through secondary
media. But so great is this mystery that we, too, may
'provisionally' at least with regard to inferior creatures
accept this generic soul of the species (or, for example, the
soul of a hive, in the case of bees); without however calling
into question the evident difference and autonomy of each
individual.

But now, faced with two conceptions of the universe, that
of the Hellenic and Thomist tradition and the conception

[1] *La Vie des Termites,* Chapter XXIII.

resulting from the intuitions of Eastern thought (which is better fitted to plumb the depths of the undeniable mysterious of the unconscious), we may find ourselves in doubt and somewhat perplexed.

Which road shall we take?

Let us accept the possibility of this mysterious soul of the world, and, consequently, the soul of the species, already anticipated by Plato.[1] Currents of thought with pantheistic tendencies will also bring their contribution to the truth.

But let us not forget the supreme synthesis of Hellenic and Christian metaphysical thought: our God, Absolute, Transcendent, Creator, who is beyond this world but who in Himself contains it. In Him is the supreme salvation of the world, the aim of the universe, the *ultimate reason* for it. He is the God of light, of understanding, in Him all things become individually distinct, from Him all things take form and life. All beings He gathers unto Himself, making each one of them radiant with its own peculiar light. Every metaphysical theory leading to annihilation must, in the final analysis, be rejected. And this—even with all our labours in the search after truth, in all our efforts to compose a synthesis—this will always be the final, decisive word.

2. *The Paradise of the Christian*

Having mentioned, as was necessary, this possible early interpretation of the soul of the world, let us try to see how eternal happiness for our little animals might be represented in the general picture of the salvation of the world.

I do not wish to enter the realm of myth. Instead I will quote St. Anselm, a mystic and at the same time a strict

---

[1] But Plato says that the two faculties, intelligence and instinct, probably stem from the same origin; coming from the same source, they are of the same nature.

metaphysician, whose wealth of language and subtlety of expression satisfy the most exacting demands of reason.

'Still Thou hidest Thyself, O Lord, from my soul, in Thy light and in Thy glory; although she is in the darkness of her shadows and her wretchedness. All around she looks, but she cannot see Thy beauty: she listens, yet hears not Thy music; smells, but perceives not Thy perfume; tastes, but recognises not Thy flavour; puts out her hand to caress, but feels not Thy smoothness. Thou hast in Thee, O Lord God, in Thine own great and ineffable way, those self-same gifts that Thou hast given to the things created by Thee; but the senses of my soul were blunted, hardened and indifferent because of the ancient malady of sin.'[1]

How do we know that the 'senses of the soul' of animals, not directly blunted and hardened by the 'ancient malady', do not participate in a keener intimacy with the root and source of all feeling, in so far as capacity is granted them to do so?

But it would perhaps be too bold to proceed further along this line of thought. Let us read on in St. Anselm. His deductions are incontrovertible, in as much as they are contained in the idea of God, in the concept of His being. (What follows might also be referred to Rupert Brooke's poem 'Heaven', quoted on page 116).

'Chapter XXV. *What good things and how many will those have who enjoy Him.*

'What good thing will he have, what will he not have, he who may enjoy this great good? Certainly he will have everything that he wants, and he will not have what he does not want. Here will be found such pleasures of the body and of the soul, such as eye never saw, nor ear never heard, nor heart of man ever thought of. . . . What do you love, O my body? What do you most long after, O my soul? Here, here is everything that you love, everything that you desire.

---

[1] St. Anselm, *Proslogion*, Chapter XII.

If beauty attracts you: here will the just shine as brightly beautiful as the sun. If speed, or strength, or freedom of the body under no restraint: these qualities will those have who are like the angels of God . . . If you wish for a long healthy life: here there is an eternity of health and eternal well-being, for the just live for ever and the health of the righteous comes from the Lord. If you wish to be well-filled: they will be full of contentment when the glory of God appears.

If you wish for true security: certainly they will all feel so assured that this good will never be lacking them in any way.

O heart of man, poor heart, heart so tried and overcome by tribulations, how happy would you be if you had all these things in abundance? Ask yourself, your inmost soul, could you ever comprehend the immense joy of such blessedness . . .'[1]

I am afraid that I am guilty of a misdeed with regard to St. Anselm: for, from all the sublime things he says in that essential and terrifying little book, the *Proslogion*, I have picked out only a few little bits here and there. And these are from among those which are nearest to the earth, earthy; those which could best serve as a kind of manual 'for the use of pussy-cats' to bring them consolation regarding their hereafter!

But my true intention is to emphasize the fact that the source of all joy, mystical, intellectual, of the senses, and of the heart, which is the Divinity, is so full to overflowing, so infinitely fruitful, that it can pour out its blessedness over all its creatures, satisfying them, transfiguring them, each according to the needs of its nature.

If God can fill with beatitude his celestial beings, he will also have a way of bringing gladness to the smallest of his creatures, who here on earth are made so happy by a single caress.

[1] *Proslogion*, Chapter XXV.

3. The salvation of the universe

But it is not only a question of 'reward' or 'compensation'. It would be short-sighted not to see how all this is in accordance with a purpose, which is the reason, for existence of each thing; a purpose which it carries within it as a plant is borne within its seed. For the 'purpose' is the true, essential, vital form of things, even taking into account all their terrestrial qualities.

And it is certain that the fate of the animal world is bound up with that of the terrestrial world; the happiness of which is to be found first of all in God (here St. Anselm confirms us), Who is the beginning of all things. But the earth itself will also be saved, in some most mysterious redemption in eternity.

Not daring to treat so difficult a theme, I will quote appropriate words from Baur, based on the testimony of St. Paul and of St. John the Apostle:

'To the resurrection of man corresponds the resurrection of the universe.

'For *the earnest expectation of the creature waiteth for the manifestation* (of the primitive glory) *of the sons of God. For the creature was made subject to vanity, but with the hope that these same created beings will be freed from the slavery of corruption, into the glorious liberty of the sons of God.*' (Romans VIII, 19, ff.)

What God had in mind in the beginning for humanity and for the whole of creation, what now lies hidden in the mud of sin, crime and death, what now groans beneath the curse of pride, will then be resplendent with purest light in the serene harmony of divine ideal and reality.

'*And I, John, saw the holy city, the new Jerusalem, coming down from God out of Heaven, prepared as a bride adorned for her husband*' (Revelation XXI, 2).

'The heaven, the new Jerusalem, the place where the Divinity appears, descends on to the earth, and earth, like a bride in her wedding dress, goes to meet her husband. From then on, the earth will no longer be the dwelling of God concealed, but of God made manifest. The superior world of the spirit and the inferior world of matter, beings and their outward appearances, heaven and earth are now one and the same thing. The earth is heavenly, matter the clearest mirror and the purest reflection of the spirit; all creation has made its way to God and partakes of His happiness; for having fulfilled its purpose, it is no longer subject to corruption or to change. It no longer grows old, but like the beauty of God Himself, blooms with eternal youth. It is for ever young, for ever new.

'The breach between material nature and spirit which sin had caused in mankind and in creation has been healed, both in individuals and in the wonderful harmony of all things. Then God will be all in all (I Corinthians XV, 28): the redemption of each individual man, of the soul and of the body, of all creation, both heaven and earth. This is the work of the Son of God, made man, in His Church! *Thy kingdom come*.'[1]

We have reached the climax where, both as regards the fate of mankind and the destiny of each creature, our capacity for knowledge is hesitant and seems to be on the point of failing us.

4. Eternity

Eternal happiness is a term for something so unfathomable, so difficult to conceive of and so awe-inspiring, that many, not bold enough to sustain the thought of it, prefer to cast

[1] *Luce dell' Anima*, Vol. III.

in their lot with those believing in nothingness. It is not the thought of happiness which is so fearful; it is the idea of eternity which has such an irresistible, and at the same time, terrifying attraction for the soul.

There is nothing else to do but take refuge in God, or better, in 'the idea of God'; and try to understand, as far as we can, what He is, and in what way 'eternity' is derived from Him. It is not an indefinite lengthening of time; but a perfection of being assumed by time, when it is given life and meaning by eternity.

In the tremendous abyss in which our consciousness flounders, there is no other way out, no other salvation (salvation which is identified with happiness, but which is, first and foremost, salvation); no other way for the wavering of our thought to be steadied than in the being of God: not only in God as if salvation had been 'given' by Him, but in Him Himself. *There is no other alternative.*

Since this sense of certainty which calms us is in the very essence of things, the universe, even in its tragic nature, seems to be essentially in a state of quiet expectancy.

*   *   *

How many times, when faced with the thought of death, we keep silent, for all that we could say seems so very inadequate. In spite of our trepidation, there is a superhuman joy in our inmost being that cannot find words.

So the mind—which recoils fearful and dissatisfied if it attempts to formulate its thoughts—is brought to rest in a reality which is far beyond it, and yet which illumines it from its source.

Single rays from the source of light frighten us. The light in itself would dazzle us; but in its total reality every doubt, every fear is stilled. All the problems we have treated, the anxieties, uncertainties, our wavering thoughts fit together into something which is everything, for it is as much our inmost being as we are ourselves, and it does not require any further justification, for it is reality. We cannot ask *why does God exist*, and with Him all the world: He exists *because He is God*.